30 AMAZING AUSTRALIAN ANIMALS

CHRISTOPHER CHENG

ILLUSTRATIONS BY
GREGORY ROGERS

RANDOM HOUSE AUSTRALIA

For J.P.R. – a really amazing Australian animal.
And for B – my favourite Australian animal. C.C.

For Harry and Pudding. G.R.

Random House Australia Pty Ltd
Level 3, 100 Pacific Highway, North Sydney, NSW 2060
www.randomhouse.com.au

Sydney   New York   Toronto
London   Auckland   Johannesburg

First published by Random House Australia in 2007

Text copyright © Christopher Cheng 2007
Illustrations copyright © Gregory Rogers 2007

The National Library of Australia
Cataloguing-in-Publication entry

Cheng, Christopher.
30 amazing Australian animals.

Bibliography.
For primary school children.
ISBN 978 1 74166 191 0 (hbk.).

1. Animals – Australia – Juvenile literature. I. Rogers,
Gregory, 1957–. II. Title. III. Title: Thirty amazing
Australian animals.

591.994

Cover illustration by Gregory Rogers
Cover design by Donna Rawlins
Internal design and layout by Donna Rawlins and Anna Warren
Printed and bound by C&C Offset Printing Co, China

10 9 8 7 6 5 4 3 2 1

Acknowledgements

Thank you to

- the folks at the NSW State Library and the Australian National Library who directed me towards the historical information sources.

- those at the Australian Museum in the many departments who answered ALL my questions – especially when I said 'Is this right?', and those who helped from the Victorian and Queensland museums.

- Healesville Sanctuary, Australian War Memorial, Sydney Olympic Authority, and NSW and Queensland National Parks and Wildlife Services.

- Special thanks to Donz for ALL your work, and to Heather, Linsay and Kimberley.

CONTENTS

FOREWORD

Why amazing creatures?

Most countries around the world like to think that their animals are *amazing* but we Australians really do have the most amazing animals … we've got mammals that lay eggs and mammals that give birth to young that look like pink jelly beans. But it is not just our mammals that are amazing. We have birds that have wings but don't fly, frogs that can survive in the desert right through years of drought, and miniature dragons that swim in the sea. We have insects whose young grow buried under the ground, coming to the surface maybe 7 years later, and, of course, we have the eight-legged wonder with a rather toxic bite. You'll meet each of these in these pages.

And because Australia is an island continent, isolated from other land masses for such a long time, most of our animals are found naturally nowhere else. We are home to the world's largest and most diverse range of marsupials, and to the largest carnivorous marsupial and the largest macropod. It is the only place where venomous snakes outnumber the non-venomous species. There are more lizards here than known anywhere else in the world. And Australia has a wide range of environments, from alpine to desert, in which Australia's animals have evolved their own solutions for survival.

Our fragile land

These amazing creatures have been surviving in this land that we call Australia for thousands and thousands of years. Unfortunately they have one huge problem – introduced animals: cats and dogs, pigs, cane toads, fire ants, not to mention you and me.

Australia's landscape is very fragile. Many of the introduced animals cause destruction of the natural environment. Their feet are often not designed for our fragile soils, and they may even eat native animals or the food our natives rely on. And we humans have spread our footprints on the land, destroying native habitats to make way for our buildings, roads, railways and farms.

What we can do

We need to find a balance where both humans and other animals can survive. Here are some simple things we all can do:

- Keep your pets well enclosed and under control so that they do not wander and compete with native animals for the limited food resources or even eat our native animals.

- Conserve our natural resources by using as little as you can of things like water, electricity, gas and paper. And don't forget to recycle!

- Investigate ways we can help our native animals survive, such as by supporting and encouraging organisations that protect our native animals (see 'How to Find Out More' on p 160).

- Find out as much as you can about our native animals and tell others about how special they are. Be an ambassador!

If only previous generations had really considered the native animal population before hunting the Thylacine to extinction. Then maybe you could actually see a living Thylacine – instead of reading about its *amazingness* in this book.

So, turn the pages, check out our amazing animals and maybe consider what you can do to help them continue to survive and flourish in this amazing land.

Christopher Cheng

www.chrischeng.com

 ¹bilby

A LONG-EARED WONDER

What animal has large ears, digs a burrow, has soft, silky grey fur and can hop? It's the bilby (*Macrotis lagotis*), sometimes called the Rabbit-eared Bandicoot or Greater Bilby. It is the largest member of the bandicoot family. An adult bilby can weigh up to 2.5 kilograms and is about the size of a small cat.

Bilbies prefer to live in hot sandy desert areas in spinifex grassland. Life in the desert isn't easy and the bilby has had to make some amazing adaptations to survive. These adaptations are so good that bilbies are the only bandicoot species that still live in the arid and semi-arid areas of Australia.

BIG EARS IN THE DESERT So why have big ears in the hot desert? Though its eyesight is poor, this creature's sensitive ears are great for hearing predators, and an excellent way to keep cool. Blood flows near the surface of the bilby's big, sparsely furred ears. The air on the ears cools the blood, which cools the bilby.

WHAT'S FOR DINNER? There's not much water to be found in the desert, so this clever marsupial gets most of the water it needs from the food it eats. This includes witchetty grubs, termites (a great source of food during times of drought), spiders and insects, plus seeds, bulbs, fungi and fruit. All this food is sniffed out by its sensitive nose and often dug up using its strong front legs and claws. Bilbies often lick seeds from the ground with their long slender tongues but they also lick up sand and soil, so a bilby's faeces (poo!) can be nine-tenths sand!

TURBO TUNNELLERS Bilbies are excellent excavators and dig deep burrows where they can escape the heat of the day, coming out after dark to feed. They may have 12 or more burrows, some spiralling down nearly 2 metres, with entrances usually hidden by termite mounds or clumps of grass. This also makes them great protection against predators.

MOTHERS AND BABIES Bilbies can live up to 11 years in captivity but possibly only 2 to 3 years in the wild. They breed when weather conditions and the food supply are favourable. The young are born in an undeveloped state only a few weeks after mating but then stay in the pouch for two months. The female's pouch has eight teats but she has only one (or sometimes two) young per litter. It's just as well that the pouch faces backwards, otherwise with all the mother's digging, she would be carrying a developing bilby plus lots and lots of dirt! After a joey leaves the pouch, usually another

litter starts suckling. But the evicted joey can still suckle for a short while.

STRUGGLE FOR SURVIVAL
Bilbies were once common, but when European settlers arrived so did their livestock and their farms which began to change the bilbies' habitat. Introduced foxes and cats also hunt the bilby, and rabbits compete for their food and burrows.

There used to be two species of bilby, the Greater Bilby and the Lesser Bilby. The smaller, the Lesser Bilby, was last seen alive in 1931 in South Australia. Sadly, it's now presumed to be extinct.

There are many bilby recovery projects in place to help boost the populations, which include breeding bilbies in captivity for release into fenced areas or onto predator-free islands.

RABBIT-PROOF FENCE

Rabbits were brought out on the First Fleet as a food supply and since then they have seriously damaged our landscape. The problem is hard to fix because they breed – like rabbits! Rabbit mothers can give birth to four or five young and have numerous litters each year.

In 1901, rabbits were approaching Western Australia from the east coast and South Australia, and the government decided to try to stop them. They began erecting what was then the longest fence in the world – the rabbit-proof fence. But the rabbits were too quick for the fence-builders, so a second fence was built and then a third, a total of over 3000 kilometres of fence! But even with three fences and regular inspections, nothing could keep the rabbits from getting close to the coast of Western Australia.

For more than 100 years, rabbit trappers have used poisons, gases, chemicals, traps, and even dug out holes. But nothing reduced the rabbit population. In the 1950s, scientists introduced the disease myxomatosis and the poison 1080 to reduce rabbit numbers. It wasn't until another disease, rabbit calicivirus, was released in 1996 and put together with the 1950s controls, that rabbit populations were put in check. Scientists are still looking for ways to rid Australia of rabbits.

HOW YOU CAN HELP At Easter time, we often exchange chocolate rabbits and eggs, but there is an Australian alternative. Many people give a chocolate bilby instead, with some profits from sales going towards bilby preservation. You could even get your school involved in fundraising for the bilby at Easter. For more information go to: http://www.easterbilby. com.au/save_bilby/fundraising.asp

The second Sunday in September is National Bilby Day, when we can promote awareness of the bilby and its struggle for survival. Why not join a local or national conservation group and get involved?

You can also be a responsible pet owner. Make sure your pets are desexed and aren't allowed to wander at night or get into areas where they may be a threat to native wildlife.

AMAZING BILBY FACTS

Bilbies don't lie down to sleep. They squat on their hind legs and tuck their snouts between their front legs, folding their ears down over their eyes.

Bilbies used to be a valuable food source for Aboriginal people. Bilbies are known as 'ninu',
'walpajirri' and 'dalgyte' in some of the many Aboriginal languages.

A Greater Bilby's body can grow to 55 centimetres in length, and its tail alone can be as long as 29 centimetres – that's nearly the length of a school ruler.

2 blue-ringed octopus

EIGHT-LIMBED WONDERS

In the coastal waters of Australia dwells the world's most lethal octopus species, the beautiful Blue-ringed Octopus. But the bright blue markings only appear when the creature is threatened. They are a deadly warning of this creature's powerful venom.

Blue-ringed Octopuses often live in coastal rock pools and shallow waters. They hide in crevices, under boulders, in old shells and even in empty bottles and tin cans that have been thrown away by unthinking people!

There are several species of Blue-ringed Octopus (*Hapalochlaena spp.*) found in Australian waters. All the species have the deadly blue markings, which scientists believe are used to

frighten away enemies. So how do they turn blue? They have special pigment cells in their skin called chromatophore cells that enable them to change colour rapidly. The blue, a rare colour in nature, is a warning sign to stay away! When they are not disturbed, and are going about their normal activities, their bodies are grey or brown, blending into the surrounding environment.

CATCHING PREY The main reason why the Blue-ringed Octopus has such toxic venom is to catch prey. Like all octopuses, it's a flesh eater, or carnivore, feeding on small crabs, shrimp and fish. It can jump and grab its prey with its long, sucker-covered arms. Its deadly venom is found in two salivary glands near its mouth, so it bites its victim with its parrot-like beak, piercing the body covering. The octopus then forces saliva into the victim and that's it – the prey is paralysed. When feeding on crustaceans like crabs or shrimp, the octopus uses its beak to rip off the hard parts of its prey – that way it can get to the soft juicy flesh, leaving behind only the hard outer shell (called the exoskeleton).

If they are too far away to jump and bite, blueys have been known to swim around crabs, and spray their toxic saliva into the water. The crab absorbs the saliva and is soon paralysed. Dinner is served!

A LETHAL INJECTION

In 1954 it was discovered that the Blue-ringed Octopus could actually kill humans. A man was bitten but he didn't even feel the bite. The venomous saliva in his bloodstream slowly paralysed him, and the nerves in his body stopped sending messages to the muscles that tell the body what to do. He became weak and uncoordinated and, even though he was conscious, he couldn't respond. Soon he found it hard to breathe and it wasn't long before his heart and lung muscles failed and he died. Thankfully only two people have been known to have died from a Blue-ringed Octopus bite. No antivenom has been developed.

BRAINS, BODY AND BLOOD Blue-rings are invertebrates, which means they don't have a backbone. Just like squids, cuttlefish, nautilus and other octopuses, they are called cephalopods, a scientific word meaning 'head foot'.

The octopus's mantle and eight long arms are attached to its head. The mantle is a thick covering of skin and muscle that protects all the internal organs. It has a large brain, which is wrapped around its oesophagus (that's the tube that runs from the mouth to the stomach. You have one too!). The octopus's mouth is found where the arms join the head. It has a beak and a jagged, chainsaw-like tongue called a radula, which is perfect for sawing though hard shells.

It has two eyes on its head. The siphon, on its mantle, is the tube the octopus uses to blow out jets of water, a great way for moving quickly through the sea. Squirting water out through the siphon propels the octopus in the opposite direction. A fast squirt and the octopus moves quickly. To change direction it simply moves the siphon. An octopus will also 'walk' with its arms along the floor of the rock pools as it searches for food.

Octopuses and other cephalopods have three hearts. Two of them pump blood through each of the two gills and the other one pumps blood around the whole body. The gills get oxygen from the water, and then the water is squirted out through the siphon.

MAKING ROOM FOR THE NEXT GENERATION

In a well-chosen shelter (maybe a discarded shell, or a rock cavity), a female will lay up to 200 fertilised eggs. The small, capsule-shaped eggs are up to six millimetres long. The mother octopus carries her eggs until they are ready to hatch. This may take up to two months, and she does not eat during this time. Females reproduce only once in their life: soon after the eggs hatch, she dies. The male also dies a few weeks after he mates with the female.

The mother might squirt her eggs, to keep them clear of rubbish. If she thinks they need protection – say from humans exploring rock pools – she may squirt her toxic saliva into the water. This can be absorbed through human skin and can make the person very uncomfortable indeed. If the mother octopus is forced to move, she can use three pairs of arms to hold onto her brood and the other pair to get through the water. About four months after hatching the young octopuses are fully mature.

AMAZING OCTOPUS FACTS

Blue-rings have lost the ability to produce the dark, cloudy ink that other cephalopods squirt into the water to escape predators. Their blue rings and bites are enough!

One Blue-ringed Octopus would have enough venomous saliva to paralyse 10 adult men.

Each one of an octopus's suckers can be moved individually. The suckers are very sensitive.

The word octopus comes from the Greek 'oktopous' – 'octo' meaning eight and 'pous' meaning feet (even though we call them arms!).

Octopuses don't have tentacles. Cuttlefish and squid, also cephalopods, have eight arms and two tentacles. These are longer than the arms and used to rapidly grab prey.

3 brumby

a poetic NEW Australian

A brumby is a feral (or wild) horse that roams free in Australia, similar to the American mustang. According to Australia's great bush poet Banjo Paterson, the word 'brumby' comes from 'boorambie' meaning horse among the Aboriginal people of the Balonne, Nebine, Warrego and Bullo rivers. Banjo Paterson's poem 'The Brumby's Run' was published in *The Bulletin* in 1895, and begins like this.

> *It lies beyond the Western Pines*
> *Towards the sinking sun,*
> *And not a survey mark defines*
> *The bounds of 'Brumby's Run'.*
> *But when the dawn makes pink the sky*
> *And steals along the plain,*
> *The Brumby horses turn and fly*
> *Towards the hills again.*
> *Ah, me! Before our day is done*
> *We long with bitter pain*
> *To ride once more on Brumby's Run*
> *And yard his mob again.*

Others say the word 'brumby' is similar to the Irish word 'bromach', which means a colt, and there were many Irish settlers in Australia's colonial past. Another possibility is that the word comes from the first record of escaped or abandoned horses. These belonged to Major John Brumby, who was a sergeant in the New South Wales Corps and also bred horses. Some say that before he sailed for Van Diemen's Land (Tasmania) in 1804 to set up the Port Dalrymple settlement, he released some horses that he could not muster into the New South Wales bush. These 'wild' horses were known as Brumby's horses, later brumbies.

One famous escape was related by Banjo Paterson in his well known poem 'The Man From Snowy River', which is about a thoroughbred, a colt, that had escaped and was running with the wild bush horses.

There was movement at the station, for the word had passed around
That the colt from old Regret had got away,
And had joined the wild bush horses – he was worth a thousand pound,
So all the cracks had gathered to the fray.
All the tried and noted riders from the stations near and far
Had mustered at the homestead overnight,
For the bushmen love hard riding where the wild bush horses are,
And the stock-horse snuffs the battle with delight.

WHERE DID ALL THOSE HORSES COME FROM?

Horses (*Equus caballus*) arrived in Australia aboard the First Fleet in 1788. Along with the military, civilians, provisions and the convict cargo there was livestock that included one stallion, four mares, a filly and a colt. Twenty years later there were more than 200 horses in New South Wales. Other horses imported from England and India arrived with the following fleets. This improved the bloodline and created a very solid working horse, perfect for Australia and for farms. For the first 100 years of European settlement, horses were essential for movement around the colony and for working on large properties. And, of course, horses carried the early explorers into the bush and beyond.

But in those early years of settlement, many properties were unfenced and horses escaped. As time went on and technology became better, other horses were released into the wild as they were no longer needed.

BRUMBIES AND THE LAND

Wild horses (as well as many other wild animals) can do severe damage to the Australian landscape. They can cause erosion at river crossings; their hard hooves compact the soil and squash the natural vegetation; and they compete with native wildlife for feed. In a good year the population of these horses can increase by 20 per cent. That is why governments are investigating the best way to manage Australia's wild horse population.

THE WALERS
Australians were known as excellent riders, but they really established a great reputation late in World War I. When the call for troops came, the Australian Light Horse was formed, made up of men from around the country, along with their horses. Some horses met army standards and were purchased; others were bought from graziers and breeders. These horses were called Walers, because many came from New South Wales (but Victorian and Queensland horses were also known as Walers). Just like brumbies, these horses were

well adapted to the rough Australian conditions: they were strong, fast animals with stamina and confidence. They could move over rough ground and didn't mind extreme weather. These horses were branded, numbered and sailed on a fleet of transport ships for the battlefields of the war.

At Beersheba, in Palestine, on the afternoon of 31 October 1917, the 4th and 12th regiments of the Light Horse began a mounted charge against their Turkish opponents across three kilometres of open rocky ground. Artillery and bullets whizzed by but most of the Walers successfully delivered their riders over the enemy's trenches and into the town.

More than 120,000 Australian-bred horses were sent to World War I and only one officially returned. Australia is an island, free of many diseases found in other countries, so we have strict quarantine laws. Because of this, some Walers were sold to the British Army as remounts, and the rest had to remain in the Middle East. Some cavalry men took their trusted mounts for one final ride, to return with just their saddle and bridle.

The Przewalksi's Horse (*Equus caballus przewalskii* or *Equus ferus przewalskii*), native to Mongolia, is the last truly wild horse. Sadly it became extinct in its native home, but zoos such as Western Plains Zoo in Dubbo, New South Wales, have successfully bred Przewalski's Horse in captivity. In May 1995, zoo-bred horses were released back into the Gobi.

AMAZING BRUMBY AND OTHER HORSE FACTS

Australia has the biggest population of feral horses in the world, some estimates say 300,000.

A horse's height is measured in hands: 1 hand = 10.2 centimetres.

When fully loaded with soldier and pack, a Waler could carry up to 150 kilograms. That's about 4 ½ ten-year-old boys.

Australia supplied over 300,000 horses to the British–Indian Army in India between 1834–1937.

4 camel

THE SHIP OF THE DESERT

Camels are not native to Australia but they have played an important role in the country's development and exploration.

The first camel was brought here in 1840. Camels were stronger than horses and bullocks, and could survive for nearly three times as long as horses without water, so they became real working animals.

Camels carried explorers across the arid continent. They transported freight and supplies, including heavy building materials, to remote settlements. When the motor car arrived in the outback, thousands of domesticated camels were released into the bush, where they rapidly bred and became feral. Now Australia has the largest population of wild one-humped camels (*Camelus dromedarius*).

EXPLORING CAMELS On 20 August 1860, the great Burke and Wills Victorian Exploring Expedition that included 27 camels embarked on an excursion to cross the continent from south to north. The expedition team had to cross deep streams so there were even air bags for the camels 'that could be lashed under their jowls, so as to keep their heads clear'. Some camels were pack animals carrying supplies; others transported the explorers; while another was an 'ambulance camel'.

In 1866, Sir Thomas Elder imported over 120 camels and their Afghan handlers from Karachi (in modern-day Pakistan). Descendants of these people are now Australians. Camel stud farms were established and operated till the early 1900s. As well as carrying explorers and their supplies, up to 30 camels could be linked together to form a camel train. These trains transported hundreds of kilograms of goods, sometimes wool bales, salt or mined ore. Camel trains also carried material required in the construction of such great projects as the Overland Telegraph Line (1870–72) between Adelaide and Darwin, or the 1750-kilometre-long Canning Stock Route (1908–10) built for transporting cattle. In 1906, Canning and eight other men, plus 22 camels, surveyed the Western Australian landscape, crossing the deserts to find suitable water supplies. Then 70 camels were used to transport material needed to build wells. Camel trains were also used in the construction of the Trans-Australian Railway (1912–17) transporting the railway sleepers and rails for the line between Port Augusta in South Australia and Kalgoorlie in Western Australia.

ABOUT CAMELS AND THE DESERT Australian camels are found mainly in central and central west Australia and are well adapted to living in arid environments. A camel gets most of the moisture it needs from plants, sucking the moisture from leaves, almost like a vacuum cleaner sucking up dirt.

Many desert plants are thorny or prickly, but this doesn't worry the camel because its thick lips and tough mouth are designed for this. The camel's split upper lip works like fingers, helping to draw food into the mouth. Strong sun and sandstorms are common in the desert, but the camel has a double row of eyelashes for protection. It also has a clear third eyelid, called a nictitating membrane, which it can draw across the eye if needed. The camel also has hair around its ears also to keep sand out.

Camels are two-toed ungulates (an ungulate is a hoofed animal) and have broad flat feet with leathery pads. When they stand, the foot pads spread. This gives them a better grip on the ground, which is perfect for travelling and not sinking in the sand. When they kneel and rest on the hot sands they are protected by the thick calluses on their knees and chest.

Camels, like giraffes, run with both legs on one side of the body moving together. It looks a bit rocky. Maybe that is why they are called ships of the desert.

A FUEL HUMP

A camel's hump does not store water. It is mostly fat and can weigh up to 35 kilograms. This fat is saved energy. When food is scarce then energy from the hump is absorbed. There are no bones in the hump so the hump can sag if a lot of energy is used.

WATER CONSERVATION Camels are great water conservers. They excrete mostly dry faeces as small round pellets and only a little very concentrated urine, which is a bit like syrup. They also catch any moisture running from their nostrils. It runs down a groove to the upper lip and into the mouth – mmm! Camels can also handle a large variation in body temperature, with their temperature able to get quite high before they need to sweat to cool themselves down. This means they don't sweat as much and so save water. Another clever camel trick is to face the sun, so that less of their body is exposed to the hot rays.

CAMEL HERDS Camels live in herds ranging in size from a few animals to several hundred. During rutting season, when camels breed, a dominant male camel, the bull, leads the herd of cows and calves, and fights off any rivals. During the summer months, the herd is led by an older female. Most bulls are solitary or roam the outback in packs. About 13 months after mating, a 40-kilogram camel calf is born – that's more than 10 times the weight of a human newborn. The baby camel drinks milk from one of its mother's two teats for up to 18 months until it is weaned.

AMAZING CAMEL FACTS

 Camel meat is eaten in Australia and people even drink camel milk.

 Feral camels can live for up to 50 years.

 Camels don't really spit – it's more like vomiting! They regurgitate their stomach contents along with lots of saliva, especially when they are threatened, annoyed or surprised.

 An average camel weighs 450 kilograms. That's about the combined weight of 6 adult men.

 Camels can lose up to 25 per cent of their body weight and still feel well.

 A thirsty camel can drink 100 litres of water in 10 minutes.

 Camels can go for 17 days without water.

 Australian-bred camels are exported for breeding, eating, racing and dairy products to places that include Southeast Asia, Canada, China and the Middle East.

5 cane TOAD

Back in the 1930s, Queensland's sugarcane production was being badly affected by two species of cane beetle because their larvae were eating the roots of the sugarcane plant. The solution? Bring in a biological control, the Cane Toad (*Bufo marinus*), an animal that would feast on these beetles and eliminate the problem … at least that's what some scientists thought.

Nearly 100 Cane Toads were imported from Hawaii in July 1935 and from these, more than 3000 were bred and released in Queensland. But instead of being a biological control, the Cane Toad itself became a pest and is now rampaging through Australian environments, taking its toll on many native animals. So how do we get rid of it? Do we bring in another predator to control the Cane Toad? Unfortunately no solutions have yet been found. Scientists are working on creating biological controls, but are now much more cautious about the animals they introduce.

GREEDY GUTS! Cane toads have voracious appetites. They eat almost anything that can fit into their mouths including small lizards, small marsupials, small birds, frogs, tadpoles (including their own!) and insects of all sorts. They eat dung beetles, which could mean an increase in the fly population (as dung beetles dispose of animal dung, in which flies like to breed). Cane Toads also eat large numbers of honey bees and that reduces honey production.

Some native animals have learnt to avoid eating the toxic glands of the toad, but for most animals that decide to feast on a Cane Toad, the venom oozing from the toad's glands makes them severely ill or even kills them. In other countries humans have died from eating Cane Toads. Soup boiled from Cane Toad eggs has proved fatal. Cane Toad venom can kill dogs, and precious native animals like quolls, snakes, dingoes and even crocodiles. Cane toads are toxic at every stage of their lives.

WHAT DO THEY LOOK LIKE? This invader is not what most people call pretty! The Cane Toad is a large, solid amphibian with dry, wart-covered skin. It is yellowish-grey, olive-brown or reddish-brown on top and pale with dark spots on its belly. The average adult Cane Toad is up to 15 centimetres long but they can grow to more than 23 centimetres. The largest recorded Queensland Cane Toad was 24 centimetres long and weighed 1.3 kilograms – the heavyweight amphibian champion of Australia (even though it's a ring-in).

Adult Cane Toads have bony heads and bony ridges that run over their eyes and meet at the nose. And the obvious lump

behind the eardrum is the parotoid gland. This is where the venom comes from. This is the Cane Toad's defence against predators. The venom oozes out or can be squirted onto the victim and can be absorbed through the eyes, mouth and nose.

THE LIFE CYCLE
It's a gooey mess. Each breeding time (perhaps once or twice a year), the females lay between 8000 and 35,000 black eggs in long ropy strands. The males fertilise them as they are laid. The eggs are covered and linked together in clear jelly. Within one to three days the eggs hatch and the tadpoles emerge and then develop for the next three weeks to five months, depending on food supply and water temperature – the better the conditions, the faster they develop. At between six to 18 months the animal is sexually mature and ready to start the cycle all over again. And considering that Cane Toads can live for up to five years in the wild, that's an awful lot of eggs produced in one toadish lifetime, though less than one per cent of these eggs survive to maturity.

MISTAKEN IDENTITY

Toads, amphibians that belong to the family *Bufonidae*, are found in most parts of the world, but Australia has no native toads, although smaller Australian frogs with short legs and chunky bodies have sometimes been confused with toads. Amphibians such as the Crucifix Toad (*Notaden bennettii*) and the Desert Spadefoot Toad (*Notaden nicholsii*) are actually frogs. The Banjo Frog (*Limnodynastes interioris*) and the Giant Burrowing Frog (*Heleioporus australiacus*) are also mistaken for Cane Toads.

The tadpoles of native frogs are usually bigger than those of the Cane Toad but the toad's tadpoles group together in huge numbers, competing with the smaller number of native tadpoles for breeding areas.

In Australia, Cane Toads have extended their range from much of Queensland, into northern New South Wales and the far reaches of Kakadu. And we now know that wherever Cane Toads are breeding, numbers of native frogs (and other animals) have declined. Cane Toads compete for food, habitat, shelters, breeding sites and they can carry disease that is transmitted to native frog populations. Not good.

TOAD WARFARE Scientists tried to use a virus from Venezuela, one of the toad's native habitats, to get rid of them. Under laboratory-controlled conditions, scientists tested the virus on the toad and also Australian frogs. Although the virus killed the Cane Toad tadpoles, it also killed the native frogs, so that wasn't the answer.

Scientists are now trying gene therapy, which means they are exploring the toad's genetic make-up. Toads, like frogs, are amphibians, which usually have two life stages – an aquatic tadpole stage and a terrestrial adult stage. If they can find a gene that stops a tadpole developing and is safe on the rest of the environment, they could release this special breed of toad into the wild. This toad would breed with wild toads, and their offspring wouldn't grow to adulthood.

Dingoes are being trained to sniff out hiding toads, just like bomb sniffer dogs. They sniff, they find, they alert humans who can get rid of the toad – but they don't touch.

Cane toads have no natural predator, so scientists have to keep working on finding a biological control. Otherwise we are going to be hopping mad for a long time to come.

BAD TIMING Had the Queensland sugarcane industry waited a few years, Australia would still be a Cane-Toad-free habitat because an insecticide was developed that controls the cane beetles. The Cane Toad had no effect on the beetles.

AMAZING CANE TOAD FACTS

They may be repellent when alive, but Cane Toad skin has proven popular in fashion accessories, such as jewellery or bags!

A Cane Toad can squirt its venom up to 1 metre.

It is estimated that there are more than 200 million Cane Toads around Australia. Yikes!

Cane toads originally come from southern North America to tropical South America.

6 cicada

nature's CHOIR

When summer comes, it's time for the Black Prince and the Forest Demon to appear alongside the first Yellow Monday. They may even argue with the Golden Knight and the Green Baron, as the Double Drummer and the Black Squeaker announce their arrivals. But never fear: the Razor Grinder and the Black Treeticker will settle any disputes. Sumptuous treats will be prepared by the Floury Baker and Chocolate Soldier and they will all join with the Green Grocer for the festival. This is not the beginning of a glorious fantasy novel. These are the names of some of Australia's most wonderful insects – cicadas.

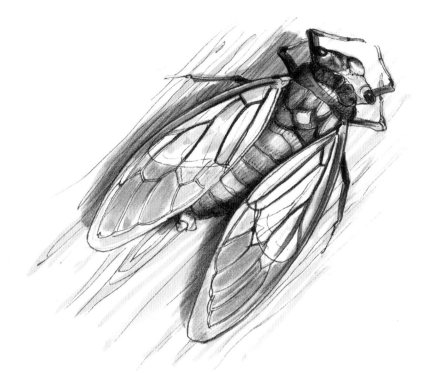

Cicadas are from the order *Hemiptera*, and most Australian cicadas come from the family *Cicadidae*.

SUMMER SONGS

Cicadas sing in summer. But it's only the males that sing – this is their mating call and each species has its own particular call. Some cicadas also have distress calls, and some have courtship calls to woo nearby females. Some songs are sung in trees in the heat of the day. Some cicadas sing at dusk, while others sing while they fly. Some cicadas, such as the Double Drummer and the Razor Grinder, gather on tree trunks and sing together so their song is intensified. This is a great protection from birds, which might otherwise feast on this delicacy as birds' ears are sensitive, so they're not likely to attack loudly calling cicadas.

A cicada's song is produced by their tymbals, ribbed membranes found on each side at the base of the abdomen. The contracting and relaxing of the muscles attached to the tymbals make them buckle or pop, like the sound when a tin can is pushed in and out. Rapid contracting and relaxing makes the song.

Some cicadas have air chambers that amplify the sound. Some can change the shape of their abdomen and others clap their wings to change sound. When a whole lot of cicadas sing together, it's very loud – too loud for many human ears! In fact, the Green Grocer is the loudest insect in the world. Its song has been measured at 120 decibels – that's as loud as a jet taking off. It's also the level when sound becomes painful to human ears. On the other hand, some smaller cicadas have such a high-pitched sound that human ears can't hear even it.

A CICADA'S LIFE Cicadas have a hollow proboscis, a built-in sucking tube, beneath their heads to pierce plants and suck out the sap. That's cicada food. Excess liquid sap goes through their body and comes out the rear end. That's cicada rain!

Cicadas are mainly tropical insects but can be found all over Australia, from snowfields to sand dunes, mangroves to grasslands and rainforests to deserts.

Cicada life starts after mating, when the female lays several hundred eggs, depositing small batches in slits she cuts in tree twigs until all the eggs are placed. After several weeks, when eggs hatch, the nymph (the immature cicada before it becomes an adult) drops into the leaf litter and then burrows underground to look for sappy roots for food. The nymph feeds on the sap, moving to another root if the sap dries up and shedding its outer layer of skin as it grows. When it's ready to hatch into its adult form, the mature nymph burrows its way to the top, only emerging from the soil when the weather is perfect for continuing the life cycle. Then it climbs the nearest tree, attaching itself to the trunk by gripping with its legs. The outer skin splits down the back and the adult cicada emerges, shedding skin for the last time. When the body has hardened and the wings dry out, the cicada then flies away, leaving its final moult on the tree. In summer, many Aussie kids collect those brown casings.

Most Australian cicadas take six to seven years to emerge from their underground homes. That's why some years there are lots more cicadas than other years. Even eggs laid at the same time might not appear as adult cicadas in the same year. The cicada then lives for a short time, from a few days to a couple of months, depending on the species.

ART AND MEDICINE LOVE CICADAS TOO

We have evidence of cicadas from ancient times, carved on wooden boxes, on brooches worn by Roman nobility, on bronze vessels, on bone combs, on coins and on gems.

They also appear on Chinese pottery, buckles, charms and amulets. Small cicadas were carved from jade and placed on the tongues of dead people, possibly to guarantee entry into the next life. Ancient Chinese kept male cicadas in small cages to listen to their pleasant song. To the ancient Chinese, cicadas were a symbol of rebirth.

More recently, Chinese herbalists have used cicadas to 'cure' many ills and aches by boiling and eating them or drinking the broth.

AMAZING CICADA FACTS

There are about 2000 species of cicada around the world. Australia has more than 220 species, and we also have the best names for them! Other interesting names include Cherrynose or Whiskey Drinker, Hairy Cicada, Bladder Cicada and the Typewriter.

Even as recently as a few decades ago, museums advertised in newspapers for cicadas (and many other insects) as more and more study was done on the diversity of the insects. Occasionally rare specimens would be brought in. Sometimes monetary rewards were even offered. This doesn't happen any more . . . but it sure was fun! The Black Prince was highly prized by children because of this.

Cicadas vary in size from 20 millimetres to 140 millimetres.

They are sometimes incorrectly called locusts. Cicadas pierce and suck when feeding, while locusts bite and chew.

Changes in weather patterns (and global warming) have meant that some cicadas are being heard outside of their traditional summer song time.

Animals that eat cicadas include birds, wasps, ants, bats and spiders . . . and sometimes people, who pull off their wings and roast them.

7 crocodile

what a TOOTHY GRIN

All Australian crocodiles are protected . . . but it wasn't always so. Up until the 1970s they were hunted; the Estuarine or Saltwater Crocodile (*Crocodylus porosus*) was nearly hunted to extinction. It's frightening to think that an animal scientists believe has survived since the time of the dinosaurs can be nearly wiped out in less than 100 years. Initially the hunting was probably to protect livestock – a sheep or cow drinking at the water's edge is a big temptation for a hungry crocodile. One sheep or cow can keep it fed for weeks.

Crocodiles were also hunted for their skins, used for handbags, shoes and even jackets. Thankfully crocodile hunting was banned and now these amazing creatures are thriving again.

BEWARE AT DINNERTIME! Crocodiles wait by the edge of the water, barely moving. So when an animal arrives at the water's edge, it is unaware that its next movement could be its last. As it enters the water, suddenly the crocodile lunges. It grabs the animal with its powerful jaws. If the animal is too big to swallow completely, the crocodile drags it under the water and begins the 'death roll', rolling over and over holding its prey firmly in its jaws until it dies. It might also vigorously shake its prey with its head, breaking off body parts piece by piece. With very large prey, the crocodile usually eats some of its catch, then leaves the remains in its underwater locker, wedged under rocks or branches, for a later meal. Some adult crocs eat only once a week during summer, less during winter.

The crocodile's cone-shaped teeth are perfect for grabbing prey but not for grinding and slicing. They tear off chunks of flesh if their food is too large to swallow. And if they happen to lose a tooth, a replacement one is waiting underneath.

Crocodiles will also eat humans. You've seen the headlines – 'Woman Taken by Croc', 'Killer Croc', 'Fatal Crocodile Attack'. A person at the water's edge (or swimming) is food. If you are in crocodile territory, make sure that you don't become lunch.

Crocodiles swim by swinging their powerful tail and strong body from side to side, their legs tucked against their bodies. They can swim long distances and stay under water for up to five hours. On land they can run quickly using their short legs.

AUSTRALIA'S CROCS The Saltwater Crocodile, or 'saltie', is the world's largest living reptile. Sometimes seen in the oceans, it prefers the swamps and the estuaries where the river meets the sea. Australia is also home to the world's only freshwater crocodile, which just happens to be called the Freshwater Crocodile (*Crocodylus johnstoni*) or 'freshie'.

Like all reptiles, crocs are ectothermic. They use their

environment to control their body temperature. Basking in the sun raises it. Resting in the shade with their mouths wide open, or lying in water, lowers it.

SALTIES   Salties are big beasts, growing to over 6 metres long and weighing over 700 kilograms, as much as a small car. During the wet season, the female lays up to 60 eggs high on riverbanks in mounds of rotting vegetation and mud that she has scraped together. This keeps the eggs warm. For the 90 days of incubation she guards her nest. When her young begin to hatch, she gently carries them in her mouth to the water where they feed on fish, crustaceans or even small mammals. She will supervise the young until they can look after themselves. That's if they make it this far.

For many animals, crocodile eggs are a delectable feast. Other reptiles like goannas, pythons and even fellow crocs will raid an unsupervised nest. Young crocodiles are also a tempting treat, especially if they stray too far from the mother's protective reach. And every year, if the nest is not built high enough on the riverbank, flooding will destroy the incubating eggs, so usually only two or three eggs survive to maturity.

FRESHIES Freshwater Crocodiles can grow up to 3 metres long and weigh over 300 kilograms. They can be active during the daylight hours but forage mostly at night. They feed on fish, frogs, crustaceans and insects. Lizards, turtles, birds or small mammals are also fair game.

At the end of the dry season, the female lays up to 20 eggs in sandbanks, which hatch within 95 days. The mother croc does not guard the nest, so these eggs are also preyed upon by other animals, especially big lizards. When she returns at the end of the incubation period, she carries her young to the water where she remains with them for just a short while before they're left to fend for themselves.

CROCODILE TEARS 'Those are just crocodile tears,' people say, when someone is pretending to cry. So what are crocodile tears? Pretend tears, in an attempt to get some sympathy. The expression came about because people used to think that crocodiles cried as they were gobbling down their victims, as if they were pretending to be sorry for eating it!

Crocodiles do cry . . . sort of. When a crocodile has been out of the water for a long time, it produces 'tears' to lubricate, or moisten, its nictitating membrane (that's the protective third eyelid in front of the eye but behind the eyelids).

SEE YOU LATER, ALLIGATOR

Crocodiles and alligators are confused for each other. So what's the difference? The main one is the different head shapes: alligators have broad U-shaped heads while crocs have narrower V-shaped heads. The fourth tooth of a croc is visible when its mouth is shut. But don't try getting close enough to look! There are no naturally occurring alligators in Australia.

AMAZING CROCODILE FACTS

Whether a crocodile hatchling becomes male or female depends on the temperature at which the eggs incubate.

To break out of their egg, young crocodiles have a caruncle (a bit like a tooth) on the tip of their snout. A few days after hatching, the caruncle is lost.

It is thought that female crocs can hear the young calling from inside the nest when they are ready to appear. Then it's excavation time.

People are more likely to be killed by bee stings or car accidents than by hungry crocodiles.

When the crocodile opens its mouth under water, a flap at the back of the throat stops water entering its lungs.

Crocodile scales are like an in-built suit of armour.

8 death adder

A deadly LURE !

Common Death Adders (*Acanthophis antarcticus*) are highly venomous, nocturnal snakes with a broad triangular head and a very short, stout body that rapidly tapers to a white-tipped tail. A mature death adder only measures about 60 centimetres long.

'Lie still, wait and wriggle the tail' – that could be the death adder's motto. When it senses approaching prey, it stays very still, sometimes partly hidden in sand or leaf litter but always with its insect-like tail exposed and twitching close to its head. A curious animal moves towards the wriggling tail, then suddenly the death adder strikes, sinking its fangs into the animal's flesh, and injects small amounts of venom. The reptile then waits patiently for its latest meal to die. Sometimes, even when it can't sense a victim nearby, the death adder might wriggle its tail hoping to attract dinner. Adult death adders like to eat small mammals and birds. Young ones eat other reptiles, like lizards.

Like most snakes, death adders have strong senses of sight and smell (they flick their tongue to taste the air). And like all snakes, they cannot hear airborne sounds, such as a bird chirping or a person speaking, because they don't have external ears. But they can feel vibrations running through the ground. When it feels threatened, this secretive reptile coils and flattens its body. It only strikes as a last resort.

DEATH ADDERS AND HUMANS
Death adders can be deadly to humans, but humans are rarely bitten. At night it is easy to mistake a death adder for a lizard and, unlike many other Australian snakes, a death adder doesn't usually slither away when approached. One man who was bitten five times by a death adder made that mistake. He suffered paralysis and a heart attack, but he was given a few vials of antivenom and survived. He was very lucky!

The death adder's venom acts on the nervous system and can cause paralysis. The nerves are attacked and breathing failure can be the result. But not everyone who is bitten needs antivenom. Some people have a mild reaction to the bite, while others have no reaction at all.

MORE SNAKY SNIPPETS
Like all reptiles, snakes are ectothermic, which means they need external heat sources to warm their bodies. So when you see a snake on the footpath or a rock or the bitumen in the middle of the day, it's because the surface is hot enough to warm its body.

Lots of people think that snakes squeeze and crush other animals. This isn't true of all snakes, although pythons do squeeze to kill. These constrictors are not squeezing to break

LIFESAVING HORSES

In 1968 the CSIRO in Australia developed polyvalent, the first anti-venom that could act against the bite of most venomous Australian snakes. Lifesaving snake antivenom is produced from injecting small but increasing amounts of venom into large Percheron horses. The horses produce antibodies to fight the venom. After about a year, blood is extracted from the horses and then the plasma, filled with antibodies, is separated from the blood. This is the antivenom. When injected into a snake-bite victim, the venom is neutralised. Thank goodness for the horses.

the bones, but to suffocate their prey. Don't forget that they swallow their prey whole, and broken bones sticking out from a body would make it very hard to digest. Bulges in snakes are usually signs of recent victims.

Snakes don't have legs so they can't run, but they *can* move quickly. They tense their incredible muscles in a wave motion to move, and many have broad belly scales, which help them to grip the ground. Most sea snakes have paddle-shaped tails to help them move too.

SNAKES AND SCALES
Scales are made from keratin, just like human fingernails and hair, and are a wonderful body covering. And when their old scaly body covering is worn out, a snake sloughs off the old and reveals the new. Snakes even have a scale that covers each eye, since they have no eyelids and cannot close their eyes like we can.

And snakes aren't slimy. The scales are dry.

SNAKES, FANGS AND VENOM Snakes aren't poisonous. Poison has to be ingested or inhaled, but some snakes are venomous. Venom is a mixture of chemicals contained in a highly developed form of saliva. Not all venoms work the same way. Some affect nerves, others muscles and others break down blood. The venom of most Australian snakes affects the nerves. When the snake bites, the victim's muscles are paralysed, it has breathing failure and other deadly problems. But not every venomous snake bite results in death.

Snake fangs can be at either the rear or front of the jaw. Front-fanged snakes, like the death adder, deliver venom through hollow syringe-like teeth. These are the most venomous snakes. Rear-fanged snakes, like the Brown Tree Snake (*Boiga irregularis*), have grooved fangs. The venom drips down the grooves into the victim. Non-venomous snakes, like pythons, don't have fangs – they have very sharp, pin-like teeth.

There has been a lot of debate about which snakes are the most venomous. The most commonly accepted measurement is not how much venom a snake has but how much venom is needed to cause death. Australia has 17 of the top 20! But don't worry – humans are more likely to be killed by cars than a snake bite.

Some snakes, like the King Brown, or Mulga (*Pseudechis australis*), bite their prey, hold on, and continuously pump venom into their victims. The Taipan, or Coastal Taipan (*Oxyuranus scutellatus*), just delivers a small jab of venom. It then lets its victim go, but the venom soon does its work. The Taipan smells its way to its prey and devours it.

SOME OTHER AUSTRALIAN SNAKES The Fierce Snake, or Inland Taipan (*Oxyuranus microlepidotus*), is Australia's most potent land snake. One bite from this reptile and the victim is quickly defeated. No human fatalities from the bite of this plain, brown-coloured snake have been reported. The largest Australian venomous snake, the Taipan, is a close relative of the Fierce Snake. The snake with the most venom is the King Brown.

AMAZING SNAKE FACTS

Australia has more species of venomous snakes than non-venomous species.

Venom is extracted from a snake by a milking process quite different to milking a cow! The snake can be made to bite through a latex membrane stretched over a beaker. The venom collected is dried and sent to a laboratory. Hundreds of milkings are needed to make a single dose of antivenom.

Most reptiles are oviparous – they lay eggs that are left to develop on their own. Some, like the death adder, are ovoviviparous – the eggs hatch internally and the young are born live. There are usually 20 young in a litter.

Constricting snakes like pythons are usually big, but venomous snakes are usually small and fast-moving.

The longest snake in Australia is the Amethystine, or Scrub Python (*Morelia kinghorni*). They average about 3.5 metres, but there are reports of this python growing up to 8 metres long. That's longer than two small cars end to end!

Sea snakes breathe air just like land snakes but they can dive for up to two hours.

⁹dingo

Australia's own WILD DOG

You've heard of the rabbit-proof fence (see page 12), but the longest fence in the world is the Dog Fence and it's also right here in Australia. Built to protect farm animals from dingo attacks, it winds for 5400 kilometres, from the Great Australian Bight, through New South Wales and Queensland's Bunya Mountains. Early European settlers put fences around their paddocks to protect their livestock. But as more and more sheep were attacked, larger dingo barriers were built. In 1946, after World War II, a single fence was established. Sheep were on the eastern side and dingoes on the western side. The fence is constructed from wooden and metal posts joined by strings of wire, then covered with tall wire mesh to keep the dingoes out. Some parts of the fence are over 120 years old. A government inspector riding a camel used to check the fence. Now they use a 4WD.

A NEW AUSTRALIAN

The dingo (*Canis lupus dingo*) is Australia's own wild dog, but it has only been here a few thousand years. Aborigines hunted with dingoes but fossil evidence tells us they did not bring them to Australia. The dingo originated in Asia and probably arrived with sea travellers and traders from Asia visiting northern Australia. The dingo then spread throughout Australia but not to Tasmania. When dingoes arrived, Tasmania was already separate from mainland Australia – and dingoes don't swim long distances.

ABOUT DINGOES

Dingoes live in small family groups but are often seen alone. The pack of up to 12 animals includes the dominant mating pair and possibly the offspring from the current year and the previous year. They spend their days roaming an area of the home territory, moving to another area every few days. Gradually, they cover the whole home range. Sometimes dingoes hunt in packs if large prey like a kangaroo is available. At other times they hunt alone.

Dingoes are more active at night, as is their diet of kangaroos, wallabies and even possums and wombats. But sheep and young cattle are also prey for dingoes. Early pastoralists considered dingoes a pest and this continues today. Dingoes terrorise sheep, harassing, biting and killing them without eating them. Outside our national parks, dingoes are not protected and can be hunted, killed and poisoned for attacking livestock.

JUST FOR DINGOES

The female dingo has just one litter of pups each year (domestic dogs have two). They mate from autumn to early winter (March to June). The female is

pregnant for 63 days and gives birth to between four and six pups. Two months later, the pups are weaned. The pups usually stay with the parents for up to one year, although they may be abandoned after a few months. The pups are born in a den, which can be a deserted wombat burrow, a hollow log or a cave. Because they are so closely related, domestic dogs pose a huge problem for the purity of dingoes. Through interbreeding, the dingo gene pool is being diluted with domestic dogs that have escaped into the bush. One of the few sanctuaries for pure-blood dingoes in their natural habitat is Fraser Island, off the Queensland coast, where domestic dogs are prohibited.

WHERE DO THEY FIT IN? Scientific names tell us a lot about the relationship of one animal to another. Dingoes have had a few scientific names. They have been known as *Canis dingo* and as *Canis familiaris dingo*, because they were thought to have evolved from dogs. But now scientists believe that dingoes are a subspecies of wolf and descendants of the Pale-footed Wolf or Indian Wolf (*Canis lupus pallipes*), so they are now classified as *Canis lupus dingo*.

Scientists once classified dogs as their own separate species, *Canis familiaris*, but not any more. DNA analysis has shown that domestic dogs evolved from the Grey Wolf (*Canis lupus*). That also makes them a subspecies of wolf, and so dogs are now known as *Canis lupus familiaris*.

These scientific names are Latin. That was the language that all scholars, including scientists understood.

Domestic dogs include the tall Irish Wolfhound and the small Chihuahua and all sorts in between, but they are all related. People have bred dogs for specific characteristics, like hunting (hounds), guarding (Dalmatians), catching rats (terriers) or warming laps (Pekinese). But no matter what size or what task, they are all related back to the Grey Wolf.

EXTINCTION Thylacines (*Thylacinus cynocephalus*) once existed on the Australian mainland, and fossils show that they were here until about 500 years after dingoes were thought to have arrived. Some people believe that the dingo contributed to the extinction of the mainland Thylacine, because dingoes competed with Thylacines for food and habitat.

Thylacines also existed in Tasmania but by the 1930s they had been hunted by people into extinction (see also chapter 28, Thylacines).

COATS OF MANY COLOURS

Over 80 per cent of pure dingoes are yellow-ginger in colour. They can also range from near black and tan to a light sand colour. Black and tan dingoes live in the forests, while the lighter sand-coloured dingoes live near sandy areas, making it easier to blend in with their surroundings when hunting.

AMAZING DINGO FACTS

 Dingoes are not only found in Australia. They also live in Thailand and other parts of Southeast Asia.

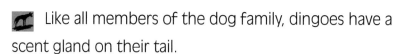 Dingoes mark their territory by scratching at the ground and urinating.

Domestic dogs bark. Dingoes howl. They howl to communicate, keep a group together and warn of intruders.

Dingoes live for about 10–12 years in the wild.

Like all members of the dog family, dingoes have a scent gland on their tail.

10 dugong

Early traditional legends describe mermaids – supernatural beings that lived in the sea – as a combination of human and fish. As time went on, they were described as having a human body and a fish's tail. But where did the mermaid legend come from?

For centuries, sailors travelled the oceans and returned to their homelands with tales of exotic creatures from distant shores, one of which was the mermaid. And no wonder. These sailors had been on the high seas for months. They may have been dehydrated, suffering from sunstroke, ill or simply lonely, when in the distance they saw creatures with smooth bodies and long flowing hair swimming through the water. Mermaids!

Of course to our eyes a dugong (*Dugong dugon*) does not look much like a mermaid. But to a lonely sailor with the sun in his eyes, these graceful aquatic human-like creatures could have captured the imagination. The long flowing hair was possibly sea grasses, which the dugong feeds on.

AN EARLY RECORD

In his book, *A Voyage to New Holland*, the explorer Captain William Dampier wrote in 1699 about a shark that his men had caught, slaughtered and ate 'very savourily'. He describes that in the mouth of one:

> . . . *we found the head and bones of a hippopotamus; the hairy lips of which were still sound and not putrefied, and the jaw was also firm, out of which we plucked a great many teeth, 2 of them 8 inches long and as big as a man's thumb, small at one end, and a little crooked . . .*

Dampier was describing a dugong. In an earlier book from 1688, *A New Voyage Around the World*, he writes of the dugong's close cousin, the manatee:

> *This creature is about the bigness of a horse, and 10 or 12 foot long. The mouth of it is much like the mouth of a cow, having great thick lips. The eyes are no bigger than a small pea; the ears are only two small holes on each side of the head. The neck is short and thick, bigger than the head. The biggest part of this creature is at the shoulders where it has two large fins, one on each side of its belly.*

In Dampier's time, there were many natural discoveries being made in yet undescribed lands like New Holland (Australia). Even though there are no hippopotamuses in Shark Bay, Western Australia, Dampier can perhaps be forgiven for thinking there were. Dugongs are more closely related to hippos and elephants than they are to marine mammals like whales and dolphins.

SIRENS OR SEA COWS? Dugongs, manatees (*Trichechus spp.*) and the extinct Steller's Sea Cow (*Hydrodamalis gigas*), are in the animal order *Sirenia*, named for the beautiful sea sirens of classical mythology – a sea nymph, part woman and part bird. Legends tell of sea nymphs bewitching sailors with their siren song, luring ships to a shattering end on rocky seabeds. Maybe the bewitching sound that entranced the lonely sailors was the whistling sound made by the large, strong male dugongs to keep their herds together.

Dugongs are large creatures, up to 3 metres long and weighing 400 kilograms. Even though they have small ears and eyes, their hearing and eyesight are excellent. Their heads are round and the mouth on their large fleshy snout faces down towards the seabed, which makes it easy for dugongs to feed on their favourite food – the young shoots of sea grasses. These grow in the muddy beds of shallow waters in northern Australia. Because they graze on sea grasses, dugongs are commonly called sea cows. Dugongs also have moustaches – heavy bristles that are excellent for helping find the sea grasses in the murky water stirred up when they tear out the whole plant, roots and all. They manoeuvre the sea grasses into their mouths with their sensitive upper lip.

SLOW AND STEADY Dugongs are slow and graceful. They steer and balance with their front flippers using them to 'walk' as they graze. They have a fluked or 'wing-shaped' tail which beats slowly up and down moving them through the water. Adult males and some elderly females have tusks. These are useful weapons for males during breeding season, when they need to fight off competing males.

Dugongs are slow breeders, giving birth under the water to only one pup about every three years. The calf often rides on the mother's back or swims nearby, never straying far. They suckle for up to 18 months from the teats close to the base of the flippers. The calf begins feeding on sea grass within a few weeks of birth and remains with the mother until it is nearly the same size as her and is fully weaned. Its place will then be taken by another pup.

AMAZING DUGONG FACTS

 Dugongs can live up to 70 years.

 These mammals are found in the tropical waters of over 40 countries in the western Pacific and Indian oceans.

Dugongs breathe through the nostrils on top of their heads but, unlike other sea mammals, they can't hold their breath for long underwater.

Tiger sharks are the dugong's main predators in Australian waters. They immobilise the dugong by biting off the tail.

11 echidna

PIN-CUSHION on legs

Only one native mammal is found right across Australia, from the wet and dry forests, and the snow-covered Alps to the deserts – not to mention most of the land in between. It is the Short-beaked Echidna (*Tachyglossus aculeatus*).

Spiny anteater, porcupine, hedgehog. Confused? Imagine how the poor echidna feels. It has a much larger nose than any of these creatures and it isn't a rodent, although some people do call it a porcupine, which *is* a rodent. (Rodents have sharp teeth like rats for gnawing, unlike the echidna.) Even though it eats ants, has a long nose and no teeth, it isn't an anteater. And even though it has prickly spines like a hedgehog, which make a wonderful defence mechanism, it isn't a hedgehog. And even though it is a mammal, like the hedgehog, the porcupine and the anteater, it doesn't live in any of the countries they live in. It lives only in Australia. These other animals are placental mammals, but the echidna is a monotreme (a mammal that lays eggs, just like the platypus).

A SPIKY LINE OF DEFENCE The spikes or stiffened hairs covering the echidna are not simply for good looks. When the echidna senses a threat and it's on hard ground it can roll into a ball of spines. If it is on soft ground, within about 30 seconds it can use all four feet to burrow straight down, flick some dirt or leaves onto its back and disappear from sight. Hollow logs and rock crevices make great defensive shelters as the echidna extends its spines and wedges itself firmly inside. No animal wants a mouthful of spines!

THE LURVE TRAIN Echidnas are solitary animals, except during breeding time. Their spines look like they might be a bit of a problem in the mating season, but echidnas seem to have it all worked out. Around July and August each year, the courting begins. At this time the waddling female echidna leaves a scent trail that the male echidnas find very attractive. It's not unusual to find four or five (or maybe ten) attentive male echidnas following a female. They form a line, biggest to smallest, head to tail processing behind the large female. These trains stay together for six weeks!

The male has worked out a clever way to mate with the female and not have his belly pierced by all those spines. Once the female echidna agrees to mate with a male, he digs a trench next to her. He waddles in alongside the female, lifts her tail with his feet and then he pushes his tail underneath while lying

on his side in his trench to mate. If there are two males they might dig trenches on either side of the female. And if there are more males then they all start digging but it is the first one in who is successful. Simple.

It is very difficult to tell the difference between a male and a female echidna. This can only be done by close observation because an echidna's sexual organs are all within the body. Male echidnas have the muscles to form a pouch just like a female but they probably can't lactate (produce milk) like a female. And male echidnas have spurs like the male platypus, although their spurs are not venomous.

ECHIDNA BREEDING An echidna's offspring is hatched from a single, sticky, grape-sized, soft-shelled egg. The tiny hairless baby uses the tiny claws on its front legs to latch onto the hairs in the mother's pouch. Like female platypuses, echidnas do not have nipples. The youngster laps up milk that oozes from the mother's milk patches. At first the young echidna does not have any spines—they start to develop at

THEY'VE GOT IT LICKED!

An adult echidna tongue can be up to 17 centimetres long, great for poking into termite mounds and licking up termites. The echidna's scientific family name is *Tachyglossidae*, which comes from the Greek, 'tachys' meaning 'swift' and 'glossa' meaning 'tongue'.

about seven weeks. This is very uncomfortable for the mother who pushes the prickly youngster away. But she still looks after the young echidna while the spines continue to develop, placing it in a temporary burrow while she forages for ants and termites, sometimes only returning every five days to feed her young. It takes six to seven months to wean them. A mother's milk is always best for young growing mammals, especially for echidnas. The milk is filled with iron-laden proteins – that can make it look pink! So next time you see a procession of spiky balls waddling along, stay quiet and do not disturb. Baby echidnas are being made.

AMAZING ECHIDNA FACTS

 Echidnas have no teeth.

 Echidnas have very strong forelimbs and claws, great for digging and busting open termite mounds.

 The echidna is a close relative of the platypus and the Long-beaked Echidna from the New Guinea highlands.

 Echidnas have fur between their spines.

Check out your 5c coins – there is an echidna proudly on display.

Echidnas can live in the wild for about 50 years.

There is a lot of dirt in the echidna's diet. It comes out in its poo.

George Shaw published the first account of the echidna in the 1790s. He thought that it was related to the South American Ant Bear.

Echidnas are good swimmers. Their long snouts make great snorkels.

The common name 'echidna' comes from an early scientific name that included the word echidna, named after the Greek goddess 'Ekhidna'. She was half reptile, half woman!

Sometimes young echidnas still in the pouch are called puggles.

12 emu

A very BIG bird

Early European settlers were amazed by the emu (*Dromaius novaehollandiae*). Governor Lachlan Macquarie was so impressed that, in 1822, he sent two emus as gifts to the Governor-General of India, the Marquis of Hastings. When Macquarie set sail from Australia back to England on the *Surry*, he wrote that voyaging with the passengers were pets that included kangaroos, swans and six emus, travelling in roomy, well-aired pens. The 'pets' were to be given as gifts to friends and patrons of Governor Macquarie back in England. Unfortunately, many of the 'pets', including one of the largest emus, died on the trip.

In 1791, John Harris, who arrived in the new colony as a surgeon, wrote that emus were swifter than the fleetest of their greyhounds. Emu eggs were described as:

> ... *a Dark Green Colour with little black specks about the Size of Pin points all over it and is Very Beautiful its about a degree larger than that of a Gooses.*

ABOUT EMUS

The emu is Australia's largest bird, standing up to 2 metres high. It has wings but it can't fly. It can run really quickly – up to around 50 kilometres per hour. The legs are also very powerful fighting tools, especially if males are fighting over females.

Emus are common throughout mainland Australia but not in dense rainforest and urbanised areas. They are highly nomadic, which means they move as they need to in search of food, water and shelter.

FATHER KNOWS BEST!

An emu's courtship is a boisterous affair. There's lots of bobbing up and down, weaving and dipping, throat drumming, grunting and fluffing of feathers.

Mating begins late in December and into January. The female flattens a platform of grass into a large nest and lays her clutch of between 7 and 11 dark green eggs (although she might lay up to 20). If it is a good season and there is plenty of rain she might lay one or two more clutches with different males. Then she leaves. He has the sole responsibility for parenting.

When the eggs are laid, the male gets broody and begins incubation before the clutch is completed. She stops mating with the male but might continue to lay eggs in the nest, which are fertilised by other males. It takes 56 days of incubation before the eggs hatch and the striped chicks appear, usually in early spring. During this time the male emu sits on the eggs, rarely leaving the nest and only standing to turn the eggs every

few hours. He doesn't eat or drink at all, drawing on his fat reserves instead. While incubating the eggs, he may lose up to eight kilograms.

Once hatched, the chicks follow the male during the day and shelter beneath his feathers at night. Chicks stay with the father for up to 18 months before venturing alone. At one year old they are at full height and at two years old they are fully mature. The father emu, having missed a breeding season, will mate again.

EGGS-CELLENT MEAL Emu eggs make a very satisfactory meal. Early settlers could create large omelettes from one emu egg. One egg can weigh up to one kilogram – that's 16 big chicken eggs! The emu egg was cracked into a bowl and allowed to separate overnight. Then the cook would skim off the oil and get cooking.

In his 1906 verse 'Santa Claus in the Bush', Banjo Paterson writes:

And there he has gathered the new-laid egg –
'Twould feed three men or four –
And the emus came for the half-inch nails
Right up to the settler's door.

. . .

Sit doon, sit doon, my bonny wee man,
To the best that the hoose can do
An omelette made of the emu egg
And a paddy-melon stew.

Emu meat was enjoyed by Aborigines. Because emus are naturally inquisitive, they were easily lured, with a twirling ball of feather and rags, to a tree. Then, from up in the tree, the emu was speared.

EMU PLUME
Emu feathers were first worn in the bands of the slouch hats by the colonial troops of the Queensland Light Horsemen in the late 1890s. In 1923, a military order stated that all Light Horsemen could officially wear the emu plume . . . as long as the military (and so the taxpayers) did not have to pay for the feathers. Today the armoured units of the Australian Army still wear the emu plume.

DOWN ON THE FARM
People have tried farming emus for Australian and international markets over the last few decades – with varying degrees of success. They are farmed for feathers, skin (leather), oil, meat and even the eggs for carving on the shells.

AMAZING EMU FACTS

🦤 Emus are good swimmers.

🦤 In good years, females can lay several clutches of eggs so they can quickly replenish the population after a drought.

🦤 Emus travel in flocks of up to 20 unless they hit fences or other barriers, then the merging flocks become a very large flock.

🦤 Emus are well adapted for wandering and feeding during the heat of the day when other animals are resting. This is because their feathers are a great protection from the sun as the black tips absorb large amounts of heat.

🦤 Emus conserve water by condensing it in their nasal passages as they breathe out.

🦤 A 1100-kilometre emu-proof fence was constructed from Esperance to Geraldton in Western Australia to keep emus out of the wheat farms. They love to eat the green shoots and later the ripe wheat, which is easily trampled by emus.

🦤 The word emu comes from the Portuguese word 'ema' which means 'crane'.

🦤 You'll find the emu on the Australian coat of arms, along with the kangaroo.

13 ghost BAT

not so GHOSTLY

If there is one animal in the animal kingdom that is grossly misunderstood then it would have to be the bat. Blind as a bat, bats in the belfry, gone batty – bats are none of these things! And the Ghost Bat (*Macroderma gigas*) is not a ghost! Let's look at some batty facts before we read about the Ghost Bat.

BLIND AS A BAT?   There is no such thing. All bats have eyes and can see, although some bats have better eyesight than others. There are two types of bats. The large bats are the megabats (*Megachiroptera*) – the flying foxes and fruit bats. The smaller bats are the microbats (*Microchiroptera*). They feed on insects, although some eat small birds and mammals.

So what about that expression 'blind as a bat'? It probably came about because bats can locate their prey even on the darkest night. Microbats do this by using echolocation. They emit a high frequency sound as they fly. The sound hits the objects and bounces back to the bat, helping it locate exactly where the prey is. It's like radar used in submarines, but bats had it first.

BATS IN THE BELFRY

If someone says that you have 'bats in your belfry' then you are supposed to be crazy. They might even say you are 'batty'. This is unfair to bats, because bats are neither crazy nor unpredictable. A belfry, usually a tall building, was where bells were stored and bats often roosted there, flying out at dusk. But bats have a definite purpose. The seemingly strange flight path that a bat might take is often in response to the pulses from their echolocation.

HANGING OUT WITH GHOST BATS

In Australia we don't have any true vampire bats but we do have a member of the false vampire bat family. Only found naturally in Australia, the Ghost Bat is the largest microbat in the world and is Australia's only meat-eating (carnivorous) bat.

Ghost Bats usually roost in colonies. At night they leave their roosting sites in caves, mines or deep cracks in rocks to hunt for their next meal, which might be large insects, lizards, frogs, birds and small mammals – even other bats like the Horseshoe and Bent-wing bats.

As well as using echolocation, which we cannot hear, the Ghost Bat uses its eyes to scan the surroundings for its prey. Once located, the bat silently swoops from above, wraps its wings around the prey and then delivers a fierce bite. It then takes the prey back to the feeding site, usually an overhanging rock or a cave to eat.

Beneath the feeding site lie the remains of its meals, even body parts, in an ever-growing pile.

BABY GHOST BATS Young Ghost Bats are hairless at birth. They feed on milk from the mother's nipples, which are under her armpits. They roost in nursery colonies and also feed on prey that the mother brings back to the roost. Soon they hunt with the mother until they become independent.

CHECKING OUT OTHER BATS Not all bats are blood-sucking carnivores. Some are sap-sucking, nectar-licking, pollen lappers, like Australia's megabats, the fruit bats and flying foxes. The Grey-headed Flying Fox (*Pteropus poliocephalus*) is the largest megabat in Australia. They roost in trees in camps that can contain thousands of bats. Like all the larger bats they have big eyes, simple ears, long noses and fox-like heads. A screeching black cloud flying above at sunset could be a flying fox colony beginning their nocturnal adventures. Flying fox mothers carry their young for the first month while they are developing their fur. Then, when furred, she leaves them in the camp at night while she feeds, before returning to suckle her young.

Of Australia's megabats the funkiest-looking bat is the Eastern Tube-nosed Bat (*Nyctimene robinsoni*), especially with its large protruding nostrils and the light-green to yellow polka dots on its wings, back and ears. When it wraps its wings around its body as it roosts in the thick vegetation, these dots give it the perfect camouflage.

'I VANT TO SUCK YOUR BLOOD'

Bela Lugosi, the actor who played Count Dracula in the original 1931 movie, never said, 'I vant to suck your blood'. (Count Dracula, based on the Transylvanian warlord Vlad the Impaler, is the literary creation of Bram Stoker.) But there are bloodsucking bats!

Vampire bats don't suck the blood from their prey. Their sharp triangular front teeth make a small cut in the skin of their victim. Then they lap up the blood with their tongue. Bat saliva has an anticoagulant that stops the blood clotting so that the bat can feast until it is full. They prey on sleeping mammals, usually pigs, cows, horses and even humans. If they can't dine for a few nights, then vampire bats will probably die.

BAT'S GOOD LUCK

In Chinese the word for bats is 'fu'. It is also the written Chinese character for luck and good fortune so bats symbolise luck, long life and happiness. An image of a bat hanging upside down means that good fortune has arrived.

AMAZING BAT FACTS

Bats are the only flying mammals.

Most bats fold their wings on the side of their bodies when resting but flying foxes wrap themselves in their wings. If they are hot they use their wings as fans.

Fruit bats are excellent flyers but do not land very neatly at all. They might crash into bushes or trees to stop or grab with their claws. Their noisy landings sometimes even start squabbles.

Fruit bats have a really important role. They disperse seeds and pollinate flowers.

Bats are found on every continent except Antarctica.

About a quarter of all mammal species are bats.

The world's smallest bat (and the smallest mammal) is Kitti's Hog-nosed Bat or the Bumblebee Bat (*Craseonycteris thonglongyai*). It was discovered in Thailand in 1973 and weighs less than 2 grams (that's about the weight of a 5 cent coin) with a head and body length of about 3 centimetres and a wingspan of less than 15.2 centimetres (half a school ruler).

The smallest Australian bat is the Timor Pipistrelle (*Pipistrellus tenuis*), which normally weighs 3.5 grams.

14 goanna

a.k.a. THE lace MONITOR

One of the biggest Australian lizards is the Lace Monitor (*Varanus varius*), sometimes known as the Tree Goanna, or simply the Goanna. It is one of more than 50 species of goannas, which are also known as monitor lizards in other countries. Half of these are found in Australia.

This large arboreal (tree-living) lizard is found in the forests of eastern Australia from Cape York Peninsula through to the Flinders Ranges in South Australia. When the weather is cool and during winter, it spends its time resting in tree hollows or other sheltered areas, under fallen trees or large rocks in burrows. In the warmer weather it actively forages for food, mainly in the afternoon.

A Lace Monitor can cover large distances in its quest for food. It has a very distinctive walk, head low to the ground moving from side to side with its long forked tongue flicking in and out, sensing the air for food. Much of its food is found on the ground and includes insects, reptiles and small mammals, but it also likes possums and nestling birds.

Trees aren't only for finding food or for shelter. They are also a means of escape. When a Lace Monitor is disturbed it spirals up a tall tree trunk on the opposite side of its pursuer, grasping with its strong claws. These claws are also very useful for excavating burrows.

GOANNA FEEDING

When a Lace Monitor catches its prey, it clamps its powerful jaws on the victim, which is eaten whole. For large prey, the monitor rips and tears its victim into bite-sized pieces. It is also an opportunistic feeder. This means that if it smells out carrion (dead meat) with its forked tongue then it will soon be eating the carcass. If it's a big carcass, other goannas will join the feast.

Human picnic areas are often good feeding grounds for Lace Monitors. Frightened humans often offer food, hoping for the goanna's hasty exit.

EASY INCUBATION

Lace Monitors are egg-laying reptiles, but rather than laying the eggs and incubating them with their bodies or using the earth like some other reptiles, they use active termite mounds, which can be up to eight degrees warmer than the soil, to do the incubation. The female monitor digs a hole in a termite nest – this might be on the ground or in a tree. Then she usually lays between 6 and 12 eggs in the hole. The termites seal up the hole in their nest and for the next six to eight weeks the eggs are incubated at just the right temperature and humidity, and are protected from

predators. Sometimes the female monitor returns to the nest and excavates her hatchlings but usually they burrow out of the incubation chamber themselves.

For males, breeding time is a contest to see who will mate with the female. They chase and battle for breeding privileges.

MISUNDERSTOOD BY MANY
Early settlers mistakenly identified this monitor as a herbivorous, or plant-eating, iguana. And early naturalists had a rather unkind view of the Lace Monitor. In the *Prodromus of Zoology of Victoria* (1878 and 1890) the Lace Lizard (which it was called then) was described as having a 'fierce and bloodthirsty disposition' and was an 'unwelcome visitor in the poultry yards'.

GOANNA OIL
Early Australian bushmen noticed Aborigines using Lace Monitor fat to dress wounds and to

soothe aches and pains, and soon they developed their own bush remedies, extracting the same fat. Goanna oil had many medicinal properties and it was claimed to be the cure for anything that ached. It was also claimed to be excellent for oiling guns!

In Queensland, the production of goanna oil, liniments and salves was soon a highly successful business. Made from purified goanna oils with herbal additives, it was marketed under the Iguana brand (possibly a link with the belief of early settlers that the goanna was in fact an iguana) and identified as an Australian bush remedy. Not even the declaration by the Queensland Government that goannas were a protected species could stop goanna oil production. Goannas were caught in New South Wales and kept in a 'goannery' opposite the factory and goanna oil was eventually trumpeted around the world.

Thankfully no goannas are harmed in the production of today's goanna oil. The 'Goanna' range of products is still sold today but doesn't contain goanna fat. Goanna oil liniment is now made of eucalyptus oil, pine oil, mint and menthol as a remedy for aches and pains.

LIVING ON IN VERSE

Joseph Marconi, maker of 'Iguana' goanna salve, was remembered by Queensland schoolchildren in their chant:

Old Marconi's dead,

Knocked on the head.

Goannas are glad,

Children are sad.

Old Marconi's dead.

AMAZING GOANNA FACTS

All Lace Monitors are carnivores, or meat-eaters.

The Lace Monitor is the totem of the Bunjalung people of northern New South Wales.

Adult male Lace Monitors are usually about 1.5 metres long, although large ones can reach 2 metres, the height of a very tall person.

Frightened Lace Monitors can run very fast. They may even run on their hind legs.

Australian monitor lizards occupy most parts of Australia, living in habitats as diverse as sandy deserts, arid rocky outcrops, or around rivers and lagoons.

Gould's Goanna (or Sand Monitor) (*Varanus gouldii*) is Australia's most widespread monitor lizard.

15 great white SHARK

Jaws, the man-eater, white death, the most feared shark in the world – it's the Great White Shark (*Carcharodon carcharias*). We might panic at the thought of them, but humans aren't normally part of their diet. Sometimes, even with their well-developed sense of smell and hearing, a shark mistakes a human surfer or swimmer for a seal, and attacks.

Great White Sharks are found in waters around most of the world, from the sub-Antarctic to the equator, inshore and offshore. They are the world's most aggressive meat-eating fish, dining on sea lions, seals, dead whales and dolphins as well as large fish, turtles and sea birds. After a large meal, the Great White Shark might not need to eat again for many weeks.

LONG-DISTANCE CHAMPION

Nicole is a tagged Great White Shark. She has swum from the coast of South Africa near Cape Town, 11,000 kilometres to the Australian coast near Exmouth Gulf in 99 days. And then she turned round and swam back!

Great White Sharks or White Sharks live for about 25 years. They weigh over 3000 kilograms (the same as about 40 adult humans) and can grow up to six metres long. They are certainly the most fearsome of sea creatures.

GREAT WHITE TEETH Great White Sharks have a lot of teeth – an awful lot of teeth – and they are constantly being replaced. Behind each row are more rows of teeth and when a front tooth is lost, the tooth behind moves forward. Thankfully Great White Sharks don't have tooth fairies. They don't have chewing teeth either. The teeth, which can be over 5.5 centimetres long, are razor sharp, triangular and serrated, perfect for biting and tearing.

GREAT WHITE CAMOUFLAGE Great whites are wonderfully camouflaged. They have a white belly and a grey back. From beneath, the white belly blends in with the surface of the water. From above the grey back blends in with the ocean. This is perfect for hunting prey, which usually never knows that the killer is there until it is too late. These sharks can also leap out of the water to grab their surprised victims. And when they are hunting they can reach swimming speeds of up to 40 kilometres per hour. Female great whites are usually larger than males.

WHAT'S FOR LUNCH?
About one per cent of all species of living fishes are sharks. There are over 370 species of sharks and 166 of these swim in Australia's waters. Sharks can be as small as 25 centimetres long. Deepwater dwellers can reach 12 metres. Some sharks swim along the bottom of the ocean eating clams and crabs. A Port Jackson Shark grabs its prey with its front pointed teeth and then crushes it with the back flat molar-like teeth. Others swim the open oceans and feast on large fish and sea mammals, often waiting for weak or older animals to stray behind the rest. Some sharks are filter feeders, taking in large quantities of water and eating the tiny animals that they strain from the water. Whale Sharks use spongy tissue to strain their plankton. Plankton is made up sea animals and plants that float in the water. The word plankton comes from the Greek word 'planktos', meaning 'wandering' or 'drifting'. Plankton is one of the most plentiful life forms on earth and is a vital part of the marine food chain.

HATCHED FROM A MERMAID'S PURSE Some

sharks are oviparous. This means they lay eggs that hatch on the ocean floor. A mermaid's purse is an empty egg case. The Port Jackson Shark (*Heterodontus portusjacksoni*) lays spiral-shaped egg cases that she pushes into rock crevices. While in the egg case the baby feeds on the yolk but when that is finished the young shark, called a pup, escapes through a slit in one end of the egg case.

Other sharks are viviparous. These sharks are nourished inside their mother, attached to a placenta (similar to mammals) before they are born, the mother providing the nourishment. An example is the Blue Shark (*Prionace glauca*).

And other sharks, like the Great White, are ovoviviparous. These sharks hatch from eggs inside the mother but are nourished from the egg yolk sac. A pregnant female Great White Shark may carry up to 14 babies. When the pups are born they are about 1.5 metres long and weigh up to 22 kilograms. Immediately they swim away from the mother – they don't want to be her next meal! Many will not survive their first year, because they will be eaten by other ravenous sharks.

AMAZING SHARK FACTS

The Great White is the only shark that can hold its head out of the water.

Many sharks hunt during the night but the Great White Shark is active during the day.

Bottles, tin cans and even hats have been found in the stomachs of Great White Sharks.

Sharks are cartilaginous fishes – their skeletons are made of cartilage, a firm, elastic and flexible substance, not bone.

Shark skin is covered by tiny, sharp tooth-like structures called dermal denticles. The skin is so rough that it was once used for sandpaper.

A shark's liver is fat and oily. It helps it float in the water.

All sharks use gills (between five and seven of them) to extract oxygen from the water.

Sharks can detect the weak electrical fields produced by all live animals.

The Whale Shark (*Rhincodon typus*) is the largest shark and so the largest fish swimming the oceans (remember, real whales are mammals). The Whale Shark has been measured at 12.65 metres long and weighs 21.5 tonnes.

The Megamouth Shark (*Megachasma pelagios*) could be described as the most unusual shark. It is not often seen and lives in the deep ocean – possibly at depths of 1000 metres. It has small hook-like teeth in its huge mouth and is a filter feeder, straining small food from the water such as plankton, shrimp and jellyfish.

16 green and golden BELL FROG

VERY patriotic!

Green and gold are true Australian colours and in 1994 a green and gold problem of Olympic-sized proportions was uncovered at an old brick pit during building preparations for the Sydney 2000 Olympic Games. This was the site planned for the Olympic tennis centre. It was also home to one of the few remaining populations of the Green and Golden Bell Frog (*Litoria aurea*). When the frogs were discovered, building work stopped. But Australia was committed to the construction. What could be done? Keep building and destroy the frog population? No way! They relocated the tennis centre and now the site is an aquatic haven for these frogs.

But how can an area that had once produced three billion bricks over 100 years become a sanctuary for an endangered animal?

SHRINKING HABITAT   It all comes back to humans. Green and Golden Bell Frogs once ranged up and down the east coast of New South Wales (especially the Southern Highlands) and into Victoria. They were so common in their natural habitat that they were the specimens students dissected in biology classes. Even in the 1960s they were common in suburban Sydney, but with the spread of urban development, more than 90 per cent of this glorious frog's natural habitat has disappeared.

But it wasn't the people sprawl alone. Scientists think that one reason the frog survived in the brick pits was that the area is free of predatory fish. Some fish love eating frog eggs and tadpoles, none more so that the introduced Mosquito fish (*Gambusia affinis*), which irresponsible pet owners have allowed to escape into the natural environment. When the tennis centre was moved, the brick pit habitat was enhanced and more frog-friendly environments were constructed in surrounding areas with freshwater ponds, boulders and suitable vegetation. Now this frog is surviving very nicely.

TADPOLES GALORE!   Green and Golden Bell Frogs lay between 3000 and 10,000 eggs each time they spawn. This egg mat floats for up to 12 hours, sometimes clinging to the plants, and then sinks. Usually two days later tadpoles appear. The tadpoles feed mainly on algae and other plant material. About two months later immature frogs 'hop' out of the water.

DID YOU KNOW . . .   This frog has a very distinctive croak, consisting of a four-part call. It sounds just like a motorbike changing gears. The male frogs call to attract the female frogs during the warmer months of the year.

The toes of the Green and Golden Bell Frog are almost fully webbed to their tips, while the fingers are unwebbed. They are skilful climbers, and able to hang onto reeds. Their colourful body patterns camouflage them well in this vegetation. Although they are part of the tree frog family, they also like the water and are strong swimmers. These frogs can be found basking in the sun in the reeds and grasses near or at the edge of streams, swamps, lagoons or even garden ponds.

Adult bell frogs are carnivorous. They feed on insects like crickets, grasshoppers and cockroaches, but will also eat any moving animal they can capture and fit into their mouth, such as small lizards. They even feed on other Green and Golden Bell Frogs. Birds, lizards, snakes and other frogs like to eat this frog too. That's the way the food chain works.

MORE AWESOME FROGS TO CROAK ABOUT

Giant Burrowing Frog (*Heleioporus australiacus*)

This frog has a great defense mechanism. It inflates its body then stands side-on, on the tips of its toes and shows the attacker how big it is, hoping that the attacker will leave it alone thinking it is too big to eat. They also ooze a creamy sticky liquid from the skin glands. Giant Burrowing Frogs are rarely in the water. They burrow straight down into the loose soil with their hind feet, corkscrew-like, until they are just below the soil surface.

Hip Pocket Frog (*Assa darlingtoni*)

This tiny frog (up to three centimetres long) has pockets on its hip. Really! When the male has fertilised the eggs (up to 18 of them) and they are ready to hatch, he places his body in the middle of the clump. The hatching tadpoles (up to five millimetres long) enter his pouches, and he carries them until the tiny frogs leave. They can even be seen growing inside the pouch! No wonder this animal is also called a Pouched or Marsupial Frog.

Turtle Frog (*Myobatrachus gouldii*)

All tadpoles swim in water, right? Wrong. This bizarre-looking frog from Western Australia lays large yolky eggs in nesting chambers up two metres deep. The soil is sandy and when it rains in their semi-arid homes, the pools of water soak into the soil or evaporate. They have short stumpy limbs to burrow through the sand. There is no aquatic tadpole stage for the turtle frog. After the egg is laid in the burrow the embryo goes through its complete development inside the egg capsule. It looks like a baby turtle without a shell.

FROG OR TOAD?

Frogs and toads are amphibians. The word 'amphibian' means 'double life'. In the early stage most young amphibians breathe through gills and live in the water.

At the adult stage they breathe with lungs, live on land and most need water to breed.

Generally frogs have smooth moist skin. They move by jumping or climbing. Generally toads have rough warty skin and they move by walking.

AMAZING FROG FACTS

 A frog's tongue is attached to the front of its mouth, not at the back like our tongues.

Frogs are excellent swimmers but if they don't have access to land they can drown.

Frogs do not give warts.

Only males croak . . . to alert females to their presence for breeding.

Frogs absorb oxygen through their moist skin. This makes them very susceptible to any change in their environment.

17 koala

AT home IN THE gumtrees

The name koala probably came from an Aboriginal word meaning 'no drink'. They nearly had it right. Koalas obtain most of the moisture they require from the leaves they eat and the rain, but if they need water, they will drink water.

When it came to allocating a name for this wonderful animal the scientists got it wrong. In 1817 the koala was named *Phascolarctos cinereus*. *Cinereus* means ash-coloured or grey, the colour of koala fur, so that works, but the name *Phascolarctos* comes from the Greek words 'phaskolos' meaning 'pouch' and 'arktos' meaning 'bear'. Koalas do have the pouch but they are not bears – they are marsupials and like all marsupials their babies are very undeveloped at birth. Baby bears, on the other hand, are well developed when they are born.

European scientists gave the koala its scientific name but at that time they knew very little about marsupials, so when they looked at koalas, they thought that of all the mammals they knew, koalas were most like bears.

In 1798 John Price was the first European to record observing a koala, which the local Aboriginals called a 'cullawine'. In 1811 George Perry published his description of what he called a 'koalo', or the New Holland Sloth:

> . . . *we are at a loss to imagine for what particular scale of usefullness or happiness such an animal could by the great Author of Nature possibly be destined . . .*

Aboriginal tribes spoke many different languages with different names for the koala, but one tribe had a word close to Perry's – 'kaola'. Other names include 'koolah', 'boorabee' and 'colo'.

FASTIDIOUS FEEDERS AND GREAT SLEEPERS!

Koalas spend at least 18 hours a day sleeping and when they wake up they eat eucalyptus leaves. They may move between trees to eat, and then it is back to sleep again. Before selecting which leaves to eat, the koala moves to the tree, sniffs the trunk with its extremely sensitive nose and then decides whether the leaves are the right ones to eat. If they are the preferred leaves the koala climbs the tree using its strong limbs, hugging the tree as it climbs and gripping the branches with its non-slip paws. A koala has two 'thumbs', three 'fingers' and non-slip pads on its palms, which makes the climb easier. There are over 500 species of eucalypts but only about 50 of these are on the koala's menu. That's why they need such a good nose to sniff out the different trees. An adult koala can eat 500 grams to

one kilogram of leaves every day, but there is not much energy in all those leaves, so they might also get a few extra nutrients from eating some soil. To conserve energy, a koala sleeps.

THE FIRST YEAR   Thirty-two days after mating (a rough and speedy act), a koala baby is born. It looks like a pink jelly bean. It makes its way from the birth canal to the mother's backward facing pouch using its partly developed front legs

STRESSED OUT?

Chlamydia is a disease that impacts on some koala populations. It is sexually transmitted and can cause a koala to become sterile, blind or suffer other illnesses. It might be stress related, occurring when koalas are attacked, are overcrowded or lose their habitat.

and claws. Then it finds a nipple and grabs on. For about seven months a joey spends all its time in the mother's pouch. For the first 13 weeks it is attached to the swollen nipple – sleeping, growing and drinking milk. At 22 weeks the eyes are open and the head pops out of the pouch. Now it is time to learn about its very special eucalyptus diet. But the joey doesn't start eating leaves just yet. Something important enters the joey's diet first – pap. This runny liquid is licked from its mother's anus. This doesn't sound very hygienic to us, but for koalas it is essential. The pap provides the bacteria that a koala needs to safely eat eucalyptus leaves – because eucalyptus leaves are toxic.

Two weeks later, from the safety of the pouch, the joey takes its first nibble of a eucalyptus leaf followed soon after by short trips out of the pouch. By about 36 weeks the joey is too big for the pouch. Instead it rides high on its mother's back eating leaves but sometimes sneaking some milk. The joey will make short trips away from Mum, but never more than a metre. Finally, at about 12 months, the joey is weaned and if another joey arrives, it is on its own. The cycle begins again.

AMAZING KOALA FACTS

 Koalas were once hunted for their fur. It wasn't until the late 1920s that the fur trade ceased and legislation was introduced to protect it because of the severe decline in koala populations.

 Male koalas have a scent gland on their chest which they rub on the trees to mark their territory.

 Males bellow to warn off other males – a call that has been described as a cross between a donkey and a pig!

 Female koalas have two nipples in their backward-opening pouch and occasionally twins are born.

 Bush fires, droughts, domestic dogs, fast cars, disease and habitat destruction are all threats to the survival of this national treasure.

 PS: Koalas are not bears!

18 koel

THE LAZY parent

Not all Australian birds spend their whole lives in one place. Some birds, like the Common Koel (*Eudynamys scolopacea*), are winged travellers. This bird flies to Australia and lives in the tall forests, woodlands and the suburbs of northern and eastern Australia. Koels arrive here for breeding during the spring and summer months and then fly back to their northern winter homes in New Guinea and Indonesia around March. Some koels may spend their lives in Australia.

The male koel is easily recognised by his glossy black feathers, with blue and green tinges, and his stunning red eyes – if he can be seen. Even though he is often heard, he usually remains hidden in the tree canopy. The smaller secretive female koel is not as glamorous as the male. She still has some glossy black feathers and red eyes, but also brown and white spotted feathers on her back and wings.

Often koels are perched alone in trees, or in small groups – especially if the female is being wooed by noisy male koel suitors. These suitors sometimes chase each other in flight, to demonstrate their mating suitability. At feeding times koel groups can be quite large. Occasionally they might be in mixed flocks with other birds.

From the tree canopy, where they spend most of their time, adult koels eat native and introduced fruits including figs and berries, as well as the occasional insect.

WHAT'S THAT NOISE?

Males are often the first to arrive at the breeding grounds where they begin their singing. Have you heard that repetitive 'cooee' from the male koel early in the morning, late in the afternoon or sometimes all through the night? Koels make some other noises including chuckles and gurgles, but the most recognised call, at least by humans, is that whistling crescendo-ing 'coo-ee' (or ko-el) that goes on and on and on! It's persistent and loud and annoys many people because it keeps them awake at night.

For early European settlers, birds like the koel were great weather predictors. When they heard the call of the koel, to them this call signalled that a storm was brewing and rain was coming. That's why they were also known as the Rainbird or the Cooee Bird.

NESTING

Koels are members of the cuckoo family and like many cuckoos parenting is a job that they totally avoid. Koels are parasites, at least for egg hatching. They do not build a nest. Instead, after mating, the female koel lays her egg

in the nest of another bird that has just laid her own (often similar-looking) eggs. The male koel provides a distraction and the female host leaves the nest to chase it away. This gives the female koel the chance to secretly deposit her egg. Honeyeaters, orioles and magpie-larks make wonderful koel host parents!

Unfortunately, the foster mother's eggs are unlikely to survive. Two or three days after hatching, the young koel evicts all other eggs and any other hatchlings. This youngster does not want any competitors. That way the foster parents, which

COOEE MATE!

So recognised is the cooee that it has become a sign of being Australian. Men used to cooee to each other in the bush, and as a welcome or greeting. Possibly the most famous cooee greetings were in 1915. During World War I, a small band of men began a march from Gilgandra to Sydney to enlist and in every town they came to they called cooee to announce their arrival. By the end of the march six weeks later more than 260 men had left their homes and were ready to volunteer to fight in the war to end all wars. This march became known as the great 'Cooee Recruitment March'. Soon many recruitment posters were emblazoned with the call 'cooee'.

look nothing like the koel chick, can devote all their time to feeding the ravenous hatchling. The koel chick will eat any food that arrives, even though it may not be part of a koel's normal diet. If there happens to be another hatchling in the nest, it will probably starve because the koel chick is more aggressive with its feeding.

Even when the hatchling has left the nest, the foster parents' job is not complete. The young koel perches on branches nearby and continues to cheep, incessantly demanding food, which the host parents continue to supply. Over the next four to six weeks the young koel doubles in size. Eventually it realises that it is not related to the host parent and leaves, following other koels to the northern wintering grounds. Next spring it will return, this time to breed.

AMAZING KOEL FACTS

 Koels are migratory cuckoos.

 Along with blowflies buzzing, cicadas chorusing and frogs croaking, the call of the koel is a sign that spring has sprung.

 In many parts of Australia the arrival of koels means the rainy season is near.

 The call of the female koel is a repetitive 'wook-wook-wook'.

 They are between 39 to 46 centimetres long.

 Other koel names include the Black Cuckoo, Cooee Bird and Rainbird. John Gould in his famous book, *Birds of Australia*, called it the Flinders Cuckoo.

19 kookaburra

THE laughing LARRIKIN

*Kookaburra sits in the old gum tree
Merry merry king of the bush is he,
Laugh, kookaburra! Laugh, kookaburra!
Gay your life must be.*

This is a round many Australian children sing in their early school years, but is the kookaburra really laughing? And what is the bird laughing about?

KOOKABURRA CALLING

Kookaburras have a range of calls but the one most people recognise is the call used to identify that an area belongs to them. One kookaburra (usually the dominant male) will begin calling and then the rest of the family joins in, raising the intensity.

And what are they doing? The kookaburras are identifying the boundaries of their territories. Soon neighbouring families begin registering their calls. A careful listener can even identify the boundaries of each family. Another call, a 'kooaa' is used when they are hanging out together.

THE FAMILY LIFE
Unusually, kookaburras don't flee the nest like most birds. Kookaburras can live for 20 years and young ones stay with the adults for four or five years. They help the family look after the following broods; incubating eggs, protecting offspring, teaching the kookaburra calls and finding up to 60 per cent of the food for the new hatchlings.

There is a very strong social order in the kookaburra world. The parents, the dominant male and female, stay together for life and they are the only ones in that family that breed. This occurs in the spring and summer months from September to January.

The eggs (usually two but up to four) are laid over a few days in an unlined hollow of a tree, branch or a termite mound. As soon as the first egg is laid, incubation begins – so the eggs hatch at different times. They incubate for 24 days and take 36 days to fledge (be able to fly). For the next 8 to 13 weeks they are fed by the parents or older siblings until they have developed their own hunting skills.

INSTANT DEATH
It's no laughing matter – a kookaburra nest can be a risky place for a chick. Like most birds, kookaburras are born as blind, tiny, flightless, pink blobs. But in some kookaburra nests the staggered hatching of the eggs poses a deadly problem for the later arrivals. Even though they are nearly helpless, that doesn't stop the chicks flopping around the nest attempting to bite with their beaks. If these blind chicks happen to latch onto another hatchling, especially around the neck, then death is the likely outcome. And the firstborn is often the victor.

A VARIED DIET Kookaburras are often seen perching on branches, waiting to pounce on the next meal passing by. They have a reputation as snake killers, but snakes are a very small part of their diet. They also feed on frogs, small mammals, birds and reptiles. Insects and other invertebrates (animals that don't have a backbone) are also a major source of food, especially during insect plagues. If necessary, kookaburras kill their prey, by smashing it against a tree branch or on the ground before swallowing it.

KOOKABURRA IMAGES Probably Australia's most recognised bird image is the Laughing Kookaburra (*Dacelo novaeguineae*), perched on a branch with its head thrown back, beak open, emitting its acclaimed koo-hoo-hoo-hoo-haa-haa-haa-haa. The kookaburra has been used many times as a symbol of Australia (see facts, pages 95–96).

NAME CALLING Before it was known as the Laughing Kookaburra, early European settlers called this bird other less flattering names. They noticed that at daybreak it cackled loudly, so it was called Bushman's Clock or Breakfast Bird. The settlers were also unimpressed by the strange calls. They thought that the kookaburras were laughing and mocking their attempts at farming so another name also became common – the Laughing Jackass. This name has appeared in many poems, stories and reports from the 1800s.

In 1862, W.A. Cawthorne wrote *Who Killed Cockatoo?* This is probably the first picture book published in Australia. Here's a sample:

Then flying very fast,
Came Laughing Jackass.
Hoo hoo hoo! Ha ha ha!
While he gobbled a snail
And wagged his big tail,
Hoo hoo hoo! Ha ha ha!

And this verse appeared in the 1871 *Young Australian's Alphabet*:

J is for jackass
A very strange bird
Whose Laugh in the forest
Is very absurd.

Australian poets also acclaimed the Laughing Jackass. Banjo Paterson wrote a poem called 'Why the Jackass Laughs' in his book *The Animals Noah Forgot*. In his poem 'Morning in the Bush', Henry Kendall uses a very different word for the kookaburra, a word he heard from the Wiradhuri Aboriginal language:

And wild goburras laughed aloud
Their merry morning songs . . .

Other Aboriginal tribes had different names, such as 'cocopura', 'cucuburra' and 'kukuburra' for the bird we call the kookaburra.

FAMOUS KOOKAS

Many companies have used a kookaburra logo.

The Widows Guild New South Wales have used a kookaburra; Olly the kookaburra was a mascot for 2000 Olympics, and the kookaburra is even on the crest of some councils. And of course May Gibbs included a kookaburra in her *Complete Adventures of Snugglepot and Cuddlepie.*

AMAZING KOOKABURRA FACTS

The Laughing Kookaburra, naturally occurring in eastern Australia, was introduced to Western Australia in 1897 and also to Tasmania.

Australia's first miniature postage stamp sheet was issued in 1928 and featured a kookaburra on a gum tree.

Kookaburras are the world's largest kingfisher, all of which have large heads, long, sharp, pointed bills, short legs and stubby tails.

Old enamel cooking stoves called 'Early Kooka' had a picture of a kookaburra with a worm in its beak on the oven door.

The logo and opening images on the *Fox Movietone News – Australian Edition* was a kookaburra, accompanied by the cackling call. The weekly newsreel began in the 1931 and lasted for forty years. Newsreels were shown at the theatres when people went to see the movies – before news on television!

The Kookaburra company, established in Australia in 1890, are renowned makers of fine cricket balls and other cricket and hockey equipment, all stamped with their brand logo of a kookaburra. The Kookaburra cricket ball is used in all one-day international cricket and 85 per cent of Test cricket matches.

In 1919–21, a square kookaburra coin was made, although it was never circulated.

Australia's men's hockey team is known as the Kookaburras.

The kookaburra is the bird emblem of New South Wales.

20 Lake Eacham
rainbowfish

magnificent LITTLE FISH

This small silvery-blue fish with orange and black stripes is Australia's most well known rainbowfish.

EXTINCTION IS FOREVER

In 1982, at Lake Eacham in Queensland, naturalists came across a freshwater fish that was similar to other fish found in surrounding lakes but not as brightly coloured as other members of the rainbowfish family. The differences were great enough for it to be named a new species – the Lake Eacham Rainbowfish (*Melanotaenia eachamensis*). At the time naturalists thought that Lake Eacham was the only place where this fish was found.

Sadly, it was not a long time from description to extinction. In a survey of the lake less than five years later, naturalists discovered that this rainbowfish had completely disappeared, presumed extinct in the wild . . . at least that was what the biologists thought.

WHEN BAD TURNS GOOD For generations, Australians have been keeping fish in aquariums and Australia's rainbowfish, including the Lake Eacham species, have always been popular pets. Lake Eacham is within the Lake Eacham National Park and so the animals were protected. During the 1970s, Lake Eacham Rainbowfish were illegally collected from the lake and kept in household aquariums. When it was found that the fish was extinct in the wild, hobbyists, who had been successfully breeding and trading the fish, bred more and more. In 1989 enough had been collected to reintroduce this rainbowfish back into the lake. Now, that's a positive outcome for an illegal activity!

Unfortunately, restocking the lake with the thousands of captive bred rainbowfish was not successful. Its predators were still swimming in the lake and were probably thrilled to have a whole new supply of the Lake Eacham Rainbowfish to eat. Within six months the captive-bred fish had disappeared.

MORE LAKE EACHAMS FOUND! Naturalists and scientists are always checking things. When they were checking the lakes and streams near Lake Eacham on a later survey, they found that there were more rainbowfish. Some were genetically the same as the Lake Eacham species (although some of them were coloured a little differently), some were of another species, the Eastern Rainbowfish (*Melanotaenia splendida splendida*), and some were hybrids, a mixture of the two. It was good news, but the mystery remained – how did the same species exist in two separate locations of unconnected waters?

HOW DID IT GET THERE? Naturalists aren't really sure. Lake Eacham is located in Queensland's Atherton

Tablelands. It is a small volcanic lake and the water that fills this lake comes not from rivers and streams that flow into the lake, but rather from the surrounding catchment area. Somehow, at some point, this rainbowfish appeared in the lake.

SOLVING THE MYSTERY The disappearance of this rainbowfish would still be a mystery if it weren't for the naturalists' surveys. When they surveyed the lake and found the rainbowfish missing, they discovered that four other Australian fish had appeared and were also swimming in the lake. These four larger fish with exotic common names, the Mouth Almighty (*Glossamia aprion*), Barred Grunter (*Amniataba percoides*), Sevenspot Archerfish (*Toxotes chatareus*) and the Bony Bream (*Nematalosa erebi*) were native to other waters in Australia. Their arrival is no mystery: they were introduced to the lake after the 1982 survey when the rainbowfish was first discovered. As a result they competed with the rainbowfish for the food supplied by the lake as well as becoming predators of the rainbowfish and their eggs, wiping them out of this lake in just a few years.

Even though this rainbowfish, or its very close relatives have been found in other lakes, it is not possible to restock Lake Eacham with its native fish until the exotic predators have been completely removed.

LAKE EACHAM LIVING
Like other similar species of rainbowfish, the Lake Eacham species feeds on algae, aquatic invertebrates and insects. The males grow to about 6.5 centimetres, with the females slightly smaller. Over several days, a pregnant female deposits her clear eggs. They are stuck to the aquatic plants by thin, sticky strings. Between seven and ten days later the eggs hatch and the young begin their life in the water.

WHAT A BLAST!

A maar is a volcanic crater. When molten hot magma and groundwater meet, steam is produced. It explodes through the surface and a crater is eventually formed. Lake Eacham was created this way.

The lake is 65 metres deep and is fed by underground springs, so it has a fairly constant water level, unaffected by drought.

AMAZING RAINBOW FISH FACTS

The Lake Eacham Rainbowfish is now listed as vulnerable rather than extinct in the wild because of populations found in nearby rivers and streams.

Males are slightly more colourful than the females.

Rainbowfish are unique to Australia, New Guinea and nearby islands.

The first rainbowfish was described in the 1800s.

Blue-eyes, the tiny fish of the genus Pseudomugil, are closely related to rainbowfish. They are found only in the waters of Australia and New Guinea.

One of the smallest rainbowfish is the Threadfin Rainbowfish (*Iriatherina werneri*) from New Guinea and Northern Australia. It averages about three centimetres in length. This fish has a fan-shaped dorsal fin while the second is very long and thin. The anal fin is also long and flowing.

21 little penguin

flying TORPEDOES

With their streamlined shape and their ability to 'fly' through the water, Little Penguins (*Eudyptula minor*) are nature's mini torpedoes. Like all penguins, Little Penguins cannot fly, but their small flippers, which are modified wings, propel them through the water at up to 8 kilometres per hour. Their short legs provide direction through water, and on land give the penguin its distinctive waddle.

CLEVER CAMOUFLAGE

The Little Penguin's feathers provide a camouflage called countershading. From the water below, the penguin's white belly feathers blend in with the light from above. The dark blue feathers on its back make it blend in with the surface colour of the water.

Penguin feathers are short, stiff and much denser than those of flying birds. Beneath them are the down feathers that trap air and insulate the bird against the cold. An added protection is the oily liquid the penguin produces, which it rubs all over its feathers to help repel the water. Preening feathers is also hugely important – feathers need to be clean to work properly.

PENGUINS ON PARADE

At sunset, a faint 'yap-yap' can be heard out to sea. Soon it is joined by another and then another, until a chorus of yappers announce their arrival, gathering beyond the waves. Now the world-famous penguin parade begins.

In the dark the Little Penguins return to their colonies on land. They arrive on shore and waddle to their burrows over sand and rocks. This is when they are most vulnerable. Their sleek bodies allow them exquisite manoeuvrability in water but on land they have to dodge feral animals: cats, dogs and foxes. Once safely in their nests they shelter for the night, resting or feeding their young.

At sunrise the parade resumes. They emerge from their burrows, head for the paths and scurry awkwardly back to the water. Some penguins come ashore every night; others remain at sea, sometimes for months.

A Little Penguin's nest can be a bowl shape at the end of a long tunnel. Other nests are beneath tussocks of grass, or under rocks and rock ledges. There may even be connecting tunnels. Little Penguins and their nests were once a common sight along the coastlines of south-east and south-west Australia. But now feral animals and the demand for waterfront housing have scattered them. Today penguins are still found in select coastal habitats of south-eastern and south-western Australia, on Tasmania and coastal islands, and also in New Zealand. They dine mainly on small school fish, squid and krill that they gather in short shallow dives.

PENGUINS ASHORE During the breeding season
males return to shore ahead of females. Their task is to reno-
vate old burrows, or dig new ones. Noisy male courtship greets
arriving females.

After penguins mate, two eggs are laid. Sometimes only one
egg survives. The penguins take turns incubating the eggs for
up to 35 days. After the eggs hatch, parents work in shifts to care
for the hatchlings. For the first two weeks one parent remains
with the hatchlings, while the other gathers food and returns to
regurgitate it for the young penguins. The next day they swap
roles. For the next five weeks both parents find food because the
young penguins are ravenous eaters. From five weeks of age,
the young penguins wait outside the burrow for the returning
parents and then at about eight weeks venture into the water.
During their first year, when they spend most of their time at
sea, young penguins may travel up to 1000 kilometres to find a

suitable colony and nesting site. If the parents have bred early in the season they may breed again.

Little Penguins moult annually. This shedding of feathers takes up to 20 days and because they can't go into the water while moulting they don't eat. So, before they moult, they build up extra body fat, sometimes doubling their weight. During moulting the penguins remain on land living off their body supplies. This is a dangerous time – if they are forced into the water they may die, because the new feathers are not waterproof.

PENGUIN JUMPERS

Little Penguins are not always formally attired in their deep dark blue and white waterproof suits. Some might be seen in black and gold or red and white, or any colour of the rainbow. Some have coloured neckbands and waistbands and stripes in all directions. These are the ones that have been rescued from oil spills.

When a penguin gets caught in an oil spill, it tries to swim to shore to preen its feathers to remove the oil. As it is preening it swallows some of the poisonous liquid. The detergents used by rescuers to clean the oil can also be deadly to penguins. So rescuers dress the penguins in these fashionable woollen jumpers. It absorbs some of the oil, stops them preening and also keeps them warm while they wait for their turn in the bathtub. They are surely the best dressed birds on parade!

AMAZING PENGUIN FACTS

Little Penguins are also known as Fairy Penguins or Blue Penguins.

There are 17 species of penguin in the Southern Hemisphere but Little Penguins are the only penguins resident in Australia.

The scientific name for the Little Penguin, *Eudyptula minor*, comes from the Greek 'eudyptula', meaning 'good little diver'.

Penguin chicks have a chipping or egg 'tooth' they use to hatch out of their egg. It's not a real tooth but a sharp bump on the top of the bill.

The Emperor Penguin (*Aptenodytes forsteri*) is the largest penguin in the world, weighing about 40 kilograms and standing just over 1 metre tall (about three school rulers end-to-end).

A penguin's beak has a hook on the end and sharp cutting edges to grasp food, which they swallow whole on the water's surface.

22 mountain pygmy-possum

a. mini MARSUPIAL

Humans can be such a problem for native wildlife. We build roads over the wildlife trails so we can zoom down to the ski fields, not worrying about the native casualties that get squashed along the way. But humans can also be the solution . . . as we have been with the endangered Mountain Pygmy-possum (*Burramys parvus*). There are possibly only a few thousand of these *amazing* animals left in the wild. They live in the snow-covered alpine and subalpine regions of New South Wales and Victoria, above 1400 metres. They are the only Australian mammals found nowhere else but here.

LOVE TUNNELS For most of the year male and female possums live separate lives scurrying among rock crevices, boulder fields and alpine shrubs. Adult females live in the best locations on the rocky slopes. Males live further down the hill. Come breeding time, these males make the hazardous trek across the roadways, attempting to avoid all the human-made obstacles in their way. For some of the possums this is the end of their migratory journey. Only when they have made it to the other side of the roadway can they consider scurrying up the hills to find the waiting females. It's a wonder they have any energy to mate at all!

When the ski runs are covered in snow they are compacted by all the skiing – not good for possum movement. Luckily humans have realised the problem. They haven't diverted the roadways or ski runs but they have done the next best thing. They have constructed rocky tunnels – 'love tunnels' – under the roadway and under some of the ski runs, so love-struck male possums can migrate between residences with relative safety.

Once breeding season is over and the young are weaned, it is back down the hill for the males, battling with mechanical contraptions again, to the safety of their home range.

TAILS AND TEETH, NESTING AND FOOD In
ski lodges, a Mountain Pygmy-possum is often mistaken for a mouse. You don't want to kill a native animal, so how do you tell the difference? The possum's second and third toes are joined, unlike a mouse's, but the most obvious difference is its curly tail. This tail has an essential task. It is prehensile, which means it can grasp things, like the thin-stemmed grasses that the possum uses for nest building. The possum's sharp premolar teeth on the side of the mouth are large and grooved, just right for cutting these grasses. They are also great for eating hard-shelled seeds and insects.

More than half of the possum's diet is invertebrates such as beetles and caterpillars. It especially likes the energy-rich Bogong Moth (*Agrotis infusa*), which is the main part of its diet during spring and summer. It also eats fruits and seeds, especially from the Mountain Plum Pine. This plant is very sensitive to fire and can take decades to recover from a bushfire. In 2003 a large bushfire in Kosciuszko National Park caused problems for the possum's diet and also affected much of the plant cover that it uses to hide from predators.

FAT POSSUMS Being a fat Mountain Pygmy-possum is very important. A fat possum has lots of stored energy, which will sustain them through the winter food shortage. In springtime, after hibernation, the possum might weigh about 40 grams but by wintertime they might weigh more than 80 grams. This possum is also a great hoarder. During winter it uses not only the energy stored in its body, but it can also eat from its hidden store of seeds and nuts. It is the only known Australian marsupial to do this.

BALLS OF FUR During winter the possum hibernates, going into a state of inactivity or torpor. It slows down its breathing and heartbeat, and reduces its body temperature to 2 degrees Celsius. That's how it saves energy. This requires a good cover of insulating snow, at least 1 metre. The possum is torpid for up to 20 days when it is very cold. Then it wakes for less than a day, maybe eating from its storage supplies, before once again resuming its 'sleep'. This cycle goes on for up to seven months. The Mountain Pygmy-possum is the only marsupial that hibernates.

THE POSSUM'S FAVOURITE FOOD

The Bogong Moth is a sweet morsel for the possum. In spring, this small brown moth migrates annually from its breeding grounds on the western slopes and plains and spends summer dormant (or resting) among rocks and boulders of the alpine peaks. Most moths are found on the mountain peaks and this is where the possums must travel to get their food.

AMAZING PYGMY-POSSUM FACTS

The Mountain Pygmy-possum was thought to be extinct until one was discovered in a ski chalet at Victoria's Mount Hotham in 1966.

Its tail is about 14 centimetres long, longer than its head and body length of 12 centimetres.

Females have one litter of four young each year. The young spend 30 days in the pouch and 35 days in the nest before weaning.

Females are known to have lived for 12 years, the longest age for any small terrestrial mammal.

Global warming is increasingly a threat. Less snow means less habitat (and many other consequences).

23 platypus

a duck DESIGNED BY a COMMITTEE

In 1798, George Shaw, a scientist at the British Museum, received a parcel containing a strange creature from the newly established colony of New Holland (Australia). It was not unusual for him to receive new animal specimens. Much of the world was unknown to Europeans, and exciting new species were being discovered everywhere, but this animal was quite extraordinary and perhaps a bit suspicious. It had the beak of a duck attached to the body of a four-legged creature covered with fur. Could this be a hoax?

Scientists had been fooled before so they had to be cautious. They had received specimens of mermaids from Asia which had turned out to be the heads and bodies of monkeys with tails of fish, expertly stitched together by Chinese taxidermists. (A taxidermist is someone who stuffs animal skins and mounts them to look as real as possible.)

But once George Shaw and other scientists closely examined their new specimen they agreed it was real. The British Museum still has the original pelt with Shaw's scissor marks where he tried to remove what he thought was the stitched-on bill. Even in his published description, he wondered if his eyes were playing tricks on him.

Of all the Mammalia yet known it seems the most extraordinary in its conformation; exhibiting the perfect resemblance of the beak of a Duck engrafted on the head of a quadruped.

WHAT'S IN A NAME?

Scientists had trouble naming this exciting new discovery. It had flat, webbed feet and was duck-like, so, at first, Shaw gave it the scientific name *Platypus anatinus* ('platypus' means flat-footed, and 'anatinus' means duck-like). But a beetle had already been named *Platypus*. So Shaw's new specimen with its duck-like snout and webbed feet was named *Ornithorhynchus anatinus* ('bird-snout' and 'duck-like'), but its common name stayed as the platypus.

Of course, Australian Aborigines had known of this creature for thousands of years with names like 'mallangong' and 'tambreet'. Early British settlers called it after animals from home: 'the water mole', 'duckbill' and 'duckmole'.

A MAMMAL THAT LAYS EGGS!

There were more amazing things to be discovered about the platypus. It took almost another hundred years before scientist William Caldwell confirmed that the platypus actually lays eggs, just like another unique Australian animal, the echidna. These animals were given their own 'order' (or group) called monotremes, meaning 'one hole'. This is because of another unique feature: unlike

other mammals, they have a single body opening used for both reproduction and getting rid of body wastes.

The female platypus lays two or three leathery, soft-shelled eggs (like reptile eggs) in her nesting burrow, which is up to 10 metres long. The eggs are the size of grapes and often stick together. The mother incubates the eggs by holding them against the lower part of her stomach with her curled up tail. Ten days later the eggs hatch and the young start to suckle like all mammals – though not *exactly* like them. The female platypus doesn't have nipples. She has patches on her belly where the rich milk oozes out for her young to lick. After three or four months the babies are weaned and emerge from the burrow.

Platypuses are very secretive and very difficult to breed

in captivity. Corrie, the first captive-born platypus, made its appearance at Healesville Sanctuary in Victoria in February 1944. It then took another 55 years for another successful birth – twins – again at Healesville in 1999, then another in 2001. The first platypus births at Taronga Zoo in Sydney were twins in 2003. Another set of twins (2005) and a single young (2006) have also been born there.

AN ELECTRIFYING DISCOVERY The platypus is an excellent swimmer. It spends much of its time in water and keeps its eyes, ears and nostrils tightly shut when swimming. So how does it find its food? This puzzled scientists for years. Then in 1985 scientists tried an experiment where they imitated the platypus's prey (or food) using shrimp tails attached to both live and dead batteries. The platypus went to the live ones. Scientists found that the platypus has special sensory organs in its bill that can pick up tiny amounts of electrical energy made by the muscles of its prey. The platypus sweeps its bill from side to side and when it 'feels' the energy of its prey, the platypus hones in, grabs it in its bill and stores the food in special pouches in its cheeks. Later it grinds the food with the horny grinding plates and ridges on its jaws.

OUCH! Anyone who studies the platypus knows to be very careful when picking up the male – he has a spiky defence; a spur connected to a venom gland which he uses for fighting other males during breeding season. The venom is extremely painful for humans but not deadly. The female platypus is born with the spur but she sheds hers during the first year.

CONSERVATION The platypus is found in rivers, lakes and streams in eastern Australia. There is an introduced colony on Kangaroo Island, South Australia. In the early 1900s the platypus was hunted for its fur but they are now protected. They are common but this could change if the water in their habitats is polluted or destroyed further by humans. If you see a platypus in the wild, watch from a distance but try not to disturb it.

A RAT WOOS A DUCK

Aboriginal legend tells that the first platypus was born after a young female duck mated with a very persuasive water rat. The baby had the mother's bill and webbed feet, and the father's legs and fur.

AMAZING PLATYPUS FACTS

 The platypus can stay underwater for up to 10 minutes.

 A chubby platypus tail is a good sign – it's where they store fat.

 Platypuses growl when they're disturbed.

 The first live platypus was displayed at New York Zoo in 1922 – the only one of five to survive the trip to America.

 In 1933, 'Splash' was the first platypus kept in captivity in Australia. A permit was issued for his capture.

 Fossils show that platypus ancestors lived in South America millions of years ago.

 Look at a 20 cent coin – you'll see a platypus!

24 redback spider

NOT creepy AND crawly

One of Australia's best-known spiders is the Redback Spider (*Latrodectus hasselti*), a close relative of America's Black Widow Spider (also of the genus *Latrodectus*). A Redback Spider is easily identified by the wonderfully striking orange or red slash on its glossy black (sometimes brown) body.

WATCH THAT TOILET SEAT!

The Redback Spider was immortalised in Slim Newton's 1972 hit song, 'Redback on the Toilet Seat':

> *There was a Redback on the toilet seat when I was there last night,*
> *I didn't see him in the dark but boy I felt his bite.*

It probably wasn't a male spider that bit the man in the toilet. Mostly it's only the female that bites. Male redbacks are only about a tenth of her size. He has fangs but they usually can't penetrate human skin.

REDBACK BREEDING

The male redback is probably unique in its mating process. He spins a special web and deposits sperm on it, which he then sucks into two palps (like hollow legs) found between the jaw and first leg. Once he's on the female's back, he stands on his head and somersaults, landing with his abdomen on the female's jaws. This is a dangerous and usually deadly activity. If the female is not ready to mate, or mistakes him for food, then this could be the end of his short life as she bites him, injecting her digestive juices into his abdomen. If she is ready to mate the male will transfer his sperm from one palp. At the same time the female might also have pierced him with her fangs. If he is strong enough he will pull away and then insert his second palp. Either way, his job is done as the female continues to eat him. She might not have to mate again for another two years.

Redback breeding time is between September and May. The female produces a small cotton-like sac, which she hangs in the web. This holds up to 300 eggs and within three weeks she is ready to place another sac. She can lay about eight sacs each season. That's a lot of redback hatchlings, but most of the spiderlings do not survive as they make wonderful food for the other young.

FEEDING HABITS

Insects trapped in their sticky webs are a major component of a redback's diet, but it will also eat other spiders and even lizards. Large female redbacks will also steal food stored in another spider's web. Only the female, which lives up to three years, spins a food-gathering web. During the summer months, males, which live for just six or seven months, might be seen lurking at the edge of the female's web in anticipation of an exciting mating time.

SILKY SPIDER HOMES

Redbacks spin their webs in dry sheltered areas under rocks or logs. They also love our human places – under eaves, floorboards, garden sheds, in junk piles, gardens and the outdoor dunny!

Their webs are spun from spider silk, which is amazing stuff. It comes from glands in the spider's abdomen. Different glands create different silks. Silk can be used for building a web, delivering sperm, holding eggs in a sac, lining burrows and catching prey in sticky nets or single threads. You can recognise a redback's web because it is tangled and messy, not a beautiful work of art like the orb-weaver's.

SPIDER BITES

Hundreds of redback bites are reported each year. Thankfully, today there is antivenom that can be injected into the victim to treat the bite.

To make spider antivenom, first you need to get venom from the spider. For redbacks this means dissecting (cutting open) the glands and tissues of the spider. The purified venom is then injected into horses, in small but gradually increasing doses. The horse produces antibodies to fight the venom. These are taken from the horse using a needle so the life-saving antivenom can be made.

A Redback Spider bite can be very painful and the person bitten may also sweat, become weak, feel sick and vomit. The best thing to do is put an icepack on the bitten area and get the person to hospital for treatment. An adult should try to collect the spider to be sure of its type.

There have been no deaths from Redback Spider bites since the antivenom has been available.

THE MYSTERIOUS MISS MUFFET

Little Miss Muffet sat on a tuffet,
Eating her curds and whey,
Along came a spider and sat down beside her,
And frightened Miss Muffet away.

Just who was Little Miss Muffet? There are a few possibilities, one being Patience, the stepdaughter of Dr Thomas Muffet, an English entomologist who wrote *The Theatre of Insects*, the first scientific catalogue of British native species. Another theory is that Little Miss Muffet symbolises Mary Queen of Scots and that the spider is John Knox, a church minister who did not agree with her religious ideas and wanted to scare her off the throne.

AMAZING SPIDER FACTS

Spiders are arthropods. They have an exoskeleton, a hard outer skeleton (rather than having bones inside, like we do).

Spiders moult – they shed their outer skeleton as they grow, replacing it with a new, larger exoskeleton.

Spiders are not insects. They have eight legs (insects have six), two main body parts (insects have three), piercing jaws (insects have chewing jaws) plus silk spinnerets (silk spinning organs).

Most spiders are nocturnal, meaning they are active at night.

A spider's silk line can be as thin as 0.004 millimetres. Some spiders create silk to cast lures, others use silk to help build a cover for their home's entrance, and others use silk to travel on the wind.

Net-casting spiders make a small web, a net, which they can stretch out to catch their prey. Jumping spiders may stalk and then jump on their prey.

Bird-dropping spiders have a wonderful method of camouflage to protect them from being eaten. They look like bird droppings!

25 RED kangaroo

AUSTRALIA'S BIG FOOT

Of all of Australia's amazing animals the most widely known is probably the kangaroo. From the old one-penny coin, the boxing kangaroo to the flying kangaroo (the Qantas logo), the kangaroo has come to signify anything Australian.

BIG RED! Kangaroos are the largest marsupials. And the largest kangaroo is the Red Kangaroo (*Macropus rufus*). Males can weigh up to 90 kilograms and stand nearly 2 metres tall. Males are usually a reddish-brown colour and females are often a bluish-grey – that's why they are sometimes called 'blue fliers'.

Red kangaroos live over most parts of central Australia and in all sorts of terrain, including scrub, grasslands and deserts. If conditions are right, the Red Kangaroo can breed all year round. Thirty-three days after mating, a hairless baby is born, looking like a pink jellybean and weighing less than 1 gram. It crawls to its mother's pouch and spends the next 235 days growing. When it leaves the pouch it continues to suckle for up to four months. By this time another young Red Kangaroo is developing on a different teat. Amazingly, the teats have different types of milk, one for the young in the pouch and fattier milk for the older joey out of the pouch.

If a female has a suckling baby, she can also have another fertilised egg waiting to develop. She delays the birth of the new offspring until the joey has left the pouch. This is called embryonic diapause.

The Red Kangaroo can survive with very little water, getting most of its moisture from the grasses and plants that it eats, but like all animals it still suffers during drought.

Kangaroos are sometimes seen as pests by farmers because they compete for food with livestock and can destroy fences when trying to jump through them.

HOP, HOP, HOP! Kangaroos belong to a group of animals called macropods, which means 'big foot'. Other macropods include wallabies, wallaroos, potoroos, pademelons, tree kangaroos, rat kangaroos and bettongs. Kangaroos have a distinctive feature – their hop. Their powerful hind legs, long feet and tail allow them to hop. In fact, the kangaroo is the only large animal that moves with a hopping motion. When it has to move slowly, for example when grazing, it uses all five limbs – two short forelimbs, two hind limbs and its tail for additional support. Amazingly, as the animal hops faster it uses less energy. Other animals use more energy to go faster. A Red Kangaroo can reach a hopping speed of over 60 kilometres per hour, and can leap as far as 8 metres and as high as 3 metres.

When they are hopping around, female kangaroos keep their joeys snug in their pouches by tightening their muscles. The muscles are loosened to let the joey out.

Kangaroos keep cool by resting in the hottest part of the day, sometimes lying under shady trees or in cool sand. Another great way that kangaroos keep cool is to lick their arms and let the moving air cool them.

EUROPEAN EXPLORERS AND KANGURUS

When Europeans first arrived in Australia they were amazed by these hopping animals. 'Kangurus' featured in many journals, reports and paintings. When reporting on how few species of land animals they had seen in Australia, Captain James Cook wrote: 'The sort which is in the greatest Plenty is the Kangooroo or Kanguru, so called by the Natives; we saw a good many of them about Endeavour River . . .' Cook and his men also discovered what the Aborigines had known for ages – that kangaroo meat is 'very good eating'.

In his journal (1768–1771), botanist Sir Joseph Banks wrote:

Quadrupeds we saw but few . . . The largest was calld by the natives Kangooroo. It is different from any European and indeed any animal I have heard or read of except the Gerbua of Egypt, which is not larger than a rat when this is as large as a midling Lamb; the largest we shot weighd 84 lb. It may however be easily known from all other animals by the singular property of running or rather hopping upon only its hinder legs carrying its fore bent close to its breast; in this manner however it hops so fast that in the rocky bad ground where it is commonly found it easily beat my grey hound . . .

The English word 'kangaroo' originated in northern Queensland. When Cook's ship *Endeavour* was being repaired, the men ventured ashore, meeting local Aborigines, the Guugu Yimidhirr people, who called the Grey Kangaroo (*Macropus giganteus*) 'kanguru'. The sailors interpreted 'kanguru' as the word for all kangaroos and wallabies, and both Cook and Joseph Banks used the word in their records. The word 'kangaroo' made its way to England and soon became part of the English language.

THE BOXING KANGAROO

In 1983 when Australia battled the United States of America for the America's Cup – the prized yachting trophy – a new 'sporting' Australian flag was unfurled. It was the boxing kangaroo. Since that time, this flag has decorated many sporting arenas where Aussies are competing. But it was not the first time that the boxing kangaroo was seen. During World War II, planes and other vehicles of the Royal Australian Air Force used a boxing kangaroo as their insignia. This image may have come about because when male kangaroos fight each other they can look like they're boxing.

In the 1800s one of the attractions at travelling sideshows around Australia was the 'sport' of boxing – between men and kangaroos. This could be dangerous, as kangaroos can kick out with their strong back legs, using their tails to support their weight. Thankfully, boxing matches between humans and kangaroos no longer occur in Australia.

AMAZING KANGAROO FACTS

A male Red Kangaroo is sometimes known as a 'boomer' – now made famous by the Australian Christmas carol 'Six White Boomers'.

Red Kangaroos are nocturnal (active at night) and crepuscular (active at dawn and dusk). They spend most of the daylight hours sleeping or resting.

Kangaroos live just about everywhere in Australia, from the rainforests all the way to arid deserts – even into the tropical areas. Red Kangaroos are generally found in arid and semi-arid areas.

Macropus rufus is from the Latin for 'big foot' and 'red'.

The kangaroo and the emu appear on our national coat of arms. They were chosen because they are always moving forwards (they can't walk backwards!).

Unlike wombats and koalas, macropods like kangaroos have a forward-opening pouch with four teats, but they usually have only one young in the pouch at a time.

Kangaroos can only move their hind feet together, except tree kangaroos, which can move each leg independently as they travel through the trees.

26 sulphur-crested COCKATOO

noisy BIRD from the LAND of PARROTS

Australia is home to over one-sixth of the world's 340 species of parrots and they cover every habitat across this vast continent. Gerard Mercator, a Belgian mapmaker who lived almost 500 years ago included in his world map a land (located near present-day Australia) called *Terra psittacorum* – the land of parrots.

We have some amazing parrots – cockatoos, parrots, lorikeets and rosellas – including the Galah (*Cacatua roseicapilla*), Gang-gang Cockatoo (*Callocephalon fimbriatum*), Glossy Black Cockatoo (*Calyptorhynchus lathami*), Little Corella (*Cacatua sanguinea*), Eclectus Parrot (*Eclectus roratus*) and the Rainbow Lorikeet (*Trichoglossus haematodus*). But one of the best known parrots is the Sulphur-crested Cockatoo (*Cacatua galerita*).

Its white-feathered body and impressive yellow crest are magnificent, but many would agree that this bird's most striking feature is its scratchy, squawky call. Its ear-piercing screech, often heard at sunrise or in the early evening, announces the cockatoo's arrival or departure from its roosting tree.

Sulphur-crested cockatoos naturally occur in the timbered forests of northern and eastern Australia and into Tasmania, as well as a colony now established around Perth. They are found in a variety of timbered environments, building nests in tree hollows. They are also popular pets, although it is sad that they are kept in cages. They can live for more than 65 years, so a cockatoo is a life-long pet and may even outlive its human.

COCKATOOS AND EARLY SETTLERS
Early European settlers in Australia referred to New Holland as Parrot Land. When Governor Lachlan Macquarie returned to England from Australia on board the *Surry* in 1822, he took a menagerie of 'pets' that included two white cockatoos 'and also several Parrots and Lowries'. These 'souvenirs' were often given as gifts. Today it is illegal to take parrots out of Australia without a permit. Sadly, because of the demand for them as pets, parrots like the Sulphur-crested Cockatoo are still found in the luggage of smugglers trying to take them out illegally. Many of these parrots die in transit.

A COLONIAL DELICACY
Early settlers had to get used to new tastes in the colony. Native wildlife provided a new dining experience, which was not always appealing to their taste buds. Newton Fowell, a midshipman on the First Fleet, wrote to his father from Sydney Cove in Port Jackson on 12 July 1788:

I forgot to mention among the birds the Cockatoo they are about the size of a large owl quite as white as Milk all over except a few yellow feathers on the top of their head which have a pretty effect they

are very indifferent food, & make a disagreeable Noise so the only handsome thing belonging to them is their Plumage.

Parrot pie was a regular dining experience for the early settlers in 'the land of parrots'. Letters home to England, journal records and memoirs identify parrot pies as being 'very good, very like pigeon'. Peter Cunningham, a convict ship surgeon wrote that parrot pies were even 'selling at a shilling a dozen'. When mapping the New South Wales coast, Lieutenant John Grant wrote that an Australian King Parrot was 'far preferable for flavour' than pigeon. For Christmas dinner in 1844, explorer Ludwig Leichhardt and his companions feasted on 'suet pudding and stewed cockatoo'. Parrot recipes in colonial cookbooks directed that the parrots be plucked and rubbed with butter, cooked alone or sometimes with other tasty treats. Parrots were a very pleasant change to the usual beef and mutton meals. How tastes change – thank goodness!

AN ARTIST'S DREAM
The vivid colours and unusual variety of Australia's wildlife provided early settlers with wonderful subjects for their art, and cockatoos were popular with painters.

There were no professional painters on board the First Fleet who arrived in Australia in 1788. The task of recording the animals and plants was taken up by those convicts and naval men who were trained in drawing and painting – skills mostly meant for drawing charts and mapping coastlines. One of the most talented of these was George Raper, midshipman on the *Sirius*. While the ship was being repaired, he did the first known painting by a European artist of the Port Jackson area. He also created a series of paintings that included his famous Glossy Black Cockatoo.

John Gould's landmark seven volume work, *The Birds of Australia* (published 1840–48), contained illustrations of all 681 of the then known species of Australian birds. One of these was the Sulphur-crested Cockatoo. Gould says:

> . . . *As may be readily imagined, this bird is not on favourable terms with the agriculturist, upon whose fields of newly-sewn grain and ripening maize, it commits the greatest devastation.*

WHAT TREE IS THAT?
Today it is not the farmers who are crying the loudest, but people in urban areas. Instead of feasting on its native diet of berries, seeds, nuts and roots, the cockie's powerful bill destroys timber decking and woodwork on houses. In the wild when they are not feeding, cockies will often be seen perched in trees biting off small branches and leaves, even shredding the bark. This keeps their beaks in good

shape and helps the trees flourish. For cockies, wooden features on houses are simply different trees.

HANGING ABOUT Cockatoos have zygodactyl feet (two toes forward and two toes pointing backward), which are perfectly adapted for climbing and holding, and for gripping branches to eat seeds while hanging upside down in trees. Sometimes cockatoos spin around on branches simply to have fun. They are nature's acrobats.

BLOWING THE WHISTLE

A flock of cockatoos feeding on the ground often have one or two others on lookout in a tree surveying the area. This is a great warning system – the cockies screech loudly if there is an intruder. Humans, too, have used this warning system. During illegal activities, such as a two-up game, someone would be hired as the 'cockatoo'. It was his job to be on the lookout for police. If they arrived, the cockie 'blew the whistle' and everyone disappeared.

AMAZING COCKATOO FACTS

The oldest authenticated Sulphur-crested Cockatoo died in London Zoo in 1982. The cocky was over 80 years old.

Sulphur-crested cockatoos originally congregated west of the Great Dividing Range but have now moved eastwards where there is more water. And pet cockatoos that have been released or escaped are now resident in the cities.

Large old trees with hollowed trunks make perfect nests for some cockatoos. If those trees are removed, the birds are likely to disappear.

Sulphur-crested Cockatoos lay up to three eggs. Both parents incubate the eggs for about 30 days before hatching.

Cockatoos are large parrots with crests. All species are found only in Australasia.

Each flock of cockatoos has its own roosting site. They fly long distances in search of food.

27 tasmanian DEVIL

an island's ICON

The Tasmanian Devil (*Sarcophilus harrisii*) may be the largest living carnivorous marsupial scavenging on the carcasses of dead animals; it may have the most spine-chilling, blood-curdling screech of any Australian animal; it may be able to snap bones apart with its vicious teeth and monstrously powerful jaws . . . but this majestic marsupial is not the devil its common name implies.

In fact people who have spent time with devils are more likely to describe them as shy and timid. Devils might look aggressive to intruders but it is more bluff than action. A devil is more likely to escape than fight – unless there's food involved!

Early Tasmanian farmers quickly grew to dislike the devil, which devoured their chickens at night. As with the Thylacine (see next chapter), a bounty, or paid reward, was introduced by the Van Diemen's Land Co., to rid farming lands of the creature. Females were worth three shillings and sixpence (35 cents), a decent sum of money in those days, while males were worth two shillings and sixpence (25 cents). Thankfully, the devils survived the trappings and poison, and in 1941 became a protected species.

A DEVIL OF A FEAST

Tasmanian Devils are more scavengers than hunters. They eat any dead or sick animal they can find. These nocturnal hunters might eat as much as 40 per cent of their body weight in one night if they are really hungry.

They are known to feast on wallabies, pademelons and, possibly their favourites, fatty wombats! Devils also like sheep and cattle as well as smaller mammals like possums. Other meals include echidnas, platypuses, frogs, fish and birds (especially chickens, if they can get into their pen). As well as eating flesh, devils also eat fur and the smelly guts and bones of their meal. They've been known to feast on the animal from the inside out – nothing is wasted, except maybe the skulls of some of the larger animals like wombats. They will have a go at anything that has a meaty smell to it – including people's clothes and shoes!

Tasmanian Devils usually hunt and scavenge alone. But many devils could be at the table if carcasses of large animals like cows or wallabies are on offer. This can become a very noisy event as they fight for the best feeding position. They push, shove, growl, yowl, scream, and even bite each other to get the best spot. Fighting is especially vicious if there is a ravenous female who has left her young in the den. Younger devils must wait until other devils have finished before they can start. At the end of a feast, a devil may curl up inside the remains of the animal for a rest. Feasting is a tiring business.

A DEVIL OF A LIFE Usually the female devil is dominant but once a year during mating season (usually March) the male is in charge. Mating lasts for up to five days.

Three weeks later a young devil emerges, just 10 millimetres long (about the size of your smallest fingernail). A mother devil can give birth to between 20–40 immature young but she has just four nipples so only the toughest four (usually less) will survive the first journey from the birth canal to the backward opening pouch and attach onto the milk supply. Devils' pouches are not large so it is not uncommon to see females ambling through the bush with the back legs of a young devil or two hanging from the pouch and dragging on the ground – a rough ride for both mother and young.

For four months the young develop in the pouch. Then for the next five months they live in a simple den, sometimes a hollow log, a small abandoned burrow or a cave. Their mother returns frequently to feed them milk (until they are five or six months old) and then to begin teaching them how to scavenge and feast out in the bush. At this stage, the young ones either ride on the mother's back or scamper by her side. Finally, ten months after mating, the young devils are sent off to start their own lives.

A DEVIL OF A DISEASE

In the early 1900s there was a dramatic decline in the number of devils, possibly as a result of disease. It also happened again in the 1950s. The devils are now in trouble again. They are developing facial tumours and dying a horrendous death. Scientists think this cancer could be transferred when devils bite each other. Devil's Facial Tumour Disease begins at the mouth but soon the devil has lumps or lesions on its face, neck and other parts of its body, and sometimes the eyes. The devil then has trouble eating and dies within about six months. A decrease in devil populations from this disease could mean an increase in the recently introduced fox, or the feral cat populations, which in turn would have a devastating impact on native animals.

AMAZING DEVIL FACTS

The Tasmanian Devil's scientific name is *Sarcophilus harrisii*. *Sarcophilus* means flesh lover, and *harrisii* is after the deputy surveyor-general who first described the devil, George Harris.

The inside of a devil's ear is nearly hairless. When they get excited or distressed their ears 'glow' in the sun as they are flushed with extra blood.

Devils were once found on mainland Australia.

Devils can travel up to 20 kilometres each night searching for food.

Devil's scats (that's poo) often contain large amounts of fur and bones. Other contents can include feathers, claws, teeth, and even boots and shoes!

Devils can run at about 13 kilometres per hour. Devils can also swim and young devils can climb well.

Males are heavier than females and weigh six to eight kilograms.

28 thylacine

Gone but NOT FORGOTTEN

On Monday 7 September 1936, the last captive Thylacine (*Thylacinus cynocephalus*) died, and with him the likelihood of anyone seeing a living Thylacine again. All that remains of this once magnificent animal, also known as the Tasmanian Tiger, is some grainy movie footage taken at Hobart Zoo of the animal listlessly roaming in a chicken-wire cage, as well as some skins, a few stuffed specimens, or photos of hunters with their dead prize. There are no known photographs of a Thylacine alive in the wild. Isn't it a pity that people won't again see the Tasmanian Tiger's amazing jaw, which could open to a width of 120 degrees, the wolf-like head, its stiff heavy kangaroo-like tail, or its black tiger-like stripes?

How did we get to this point where a remarkable marsupial, once common in Tasmania, is now no longer with us? For that explanation we have to look into our history. When Europeans settled in Tasmania in 1803 the Thylacine was common. This nocturnal hunter was frequently sighted. It was the largest living carnivorous (meat-eating) marsupial and should have been worthy of excitement not extermination. But it wasn't.

A DEATH SENTENCE   Sheep farming was introduced into Tasmania early in the 1800s. Sheep were a tempting treat for Thylacines, and they were possibly easier to kill than their usual meal of wallabies or other small animals. Now they had mutton to feast on. More and more sheep were slaughtered, although not necessarily by Thylacines. The growing population of wild dogs were predators too. More and more farmers pressed to get rid of Thylacines. So in 1830 the Van Diemen's Land Co. put a bounty (a paid reward) on the head of the Thylacine.

A dramatic reduction in the number of Thylacines must have been already obvious by the middle 1850s. Even the famous naturalist John Gould, in his book *The Mammals of Australia, 1845–1863*, predicted the end of the Thylacine when he wrote:

> *When the comparatively small island of Tasmania becomes more densely populated, and its primitive forests are intersected with roads from the eastern to the western coast, the numbers of this singular animal will speedily diminish, extermination will have its full sway, and it will then, like the Wolf in England and Scotland, be recorded as an animal of the past.*

In 1888 the Tasmanian parliament placed an additional bounty of £1 on an adult and ten shillings on each pup. The combined bounties were devastatingly effective because by the early 1900s few bounties were being paid. By the time the bounty was removed in 1909 over 2000 bounties had been

paid. Many more Thylacines were killed and many of the skins went to tanneries and were exported. By that time, sighting the Thylacine was uncommon. But worse was to come.

Already greatly reduced in number by the slaughter, the remaining Thylacines were probably hit with a fatal disease, so seeing a Thylacine now became extremely rare. Even so, urgent action wasn't taken to reduce the possibility of extinction. The last wild Thylacine was probably shot in 1930.

TIGER ON DISPLAY

By then zoos around the world wanted to display this tiger-like marsupial. Thylacines were on display in London's Regent Park Zoo (the last one purchased for £150 in 1926). In 1933 Hobart Zoo purchased its last Thylacine, caught in the Florentine Valley. Sydney's Taronga Zoo and the Bronx Zoo, New York, also displayed the Thylacine.

But eventually the last captive Thylacine died, possibly of exposure as the day shift keeper might have forgotten to lock it up in its hut the night before. It is a sad irony that the Thylacine was only added to the endangered wildlife list *after* the death of this last captive specimen. It was too little too late. This marsupial was probably already extinct.

Since 1936 there have been hundreds of claimed sightings of the Thylacine in Tasmania and as far away as the Northern Territory but searches have been unsuccessful. No concrete evidence, such as footprints, scats, or specimens have been found. And it is amazing that there are no authenticated photographs of the animals that are sighted.

CAN THYLACINES BE CLONED?

Cloning is the process of making an identical copy of something. In living things, cloning involves creating a copy using special material called DNA from the original animal. DNA is like building blocks with an instruction booklet of how that living thing goes together.

So could a Thylacine be cloned? This is a question that has caused much discussion in recent years. Dolly the sheep was cloned, and also many other animals, so why not a Thylacine? Scientists still hold Thylacine DNA material. Many scientists agree that cloning is possible, but is it worthwhile? A successful cloning would be great but there would only be one. And the components of the DNA from which the cloned specimen would be created are very old. The specimen, a young Thylacine pup, has been preserved in alcohol since 1866. This makes the process even more difficult. The issue of cloning creates a lot of discussion and argument!

AMAZING THYLACINE FACTS

Thylacines weren't *officially* classified as extinct until 1986, 50 years after the last captive Thylacine died.

Aboriginal rock paintings and fossil remains show that the Thylacine was once on mainland Australia. Competition with the dingo (which never made it to Tasmania) might have caused its mainland extinction.

The Tasmanian coat of arms has a shield supported by two Tasmanian Tigers.

Thylacines lived in zoos for up to nine years. No Thylacine was ever bred in captivity.

The Tasmanian Tiger's fur was sandy brown, coarse with 15 to 20 black stripes.

The scientific name (*Thylacinus cynocephalus*) means dog-headed pouched dog or is sometimes translated as 'pouched dog with wolf's head'.

29 WEEDY SEADRAGON

floating SEAWEED

Named after the dragons of Chinese legends, these amazing creatures are dragons in miniature, growing to about 46cm, and are only found in ocean waters of southern Australia. Adult Weedy Seadragons (*Phyllopteryx taeniolatus*) are usually reddish with yellow spots and purple-blue stripes, and have pipe-shaped snouts. But their main costume is their leaf-like appendages which make Weedy Seadragons look like swaying seaweed, keeping them hidden among the seaweed-covered rocky reefs where it is found.

THE DAD GIVES BIRTH! It's a wonderful life being a male seadragon, swimming around in the temperate water, sucking up plankton, larval fish or mysid (small shrimp-like crustaceans), fertilising eggs and watching your young swim away after birth. But male seadragons do more than watch. Unlike most other animals, it is the male seadragon that carries and incubates the eggs. The male seadragon becomes pregnant and the male dragon 'gives birth' to the baby seadragons.

With the approach of spring, male and female seadragons pair off and begin their courtship. During mating, the female seadragon places 100–250 bright pink eggs on the underside of the male seadragon's tail, into the brood patch. Once her job is done, she swims away and the rest is up to the male.

The brood patch contains small pits or egg-cup suction caps, each holding an egg. The male fertilises and then nourishes the eggs for up to eight weeks while they develop. Then hatching takes a while. Over a number of days, fully formed young seadragons emerge from the eggs, one or two at a time. They hang their tails out of the eggs, for up to six hours, eventually wriggling to freedom. The male seadragon spreads his offspring as he swims through the waters. For the first two days the baby seadragon obtains nourishment from the yolk sac but then it must find its own food. The young dragons are fast-growing, reaching full size after two years.

Once free of his parental responsibilities, the male seadragon has time for a second incubation in the one breeding season.

TUBE-SNOUTED COUSINS
Weedies belong to the family of Syngnthids (Latin for tube-snouted) that includes seahorses, pipehorses and pipefish. Syngnathids are long, slender fish with bony plates around their bodies. The family name describes their tube-shaped mouth. Seadragons don't have teeth so they suck in their food, along with some water. They do this by expanding a joint on the lower part of their snout, which makes a suction force that pulls in the food.

Seadragons and seahorses may look quite similar but there

are some important differences. Unlike seahorses, seadragons don't have a pouch for rearing their young but carry the eggs on their tails until they hatch. Also seadragons can't curl their tails, but seahorses have prehensile tails, which means they can curl their tail to hold onto objects such as blades of seagrass.

The Weedy Seadragon is closely related to the Leafy Seadragon (*Phycodurus eques*) which has even more leaf-like appendages but is usually smaller than its weedy cousin.

CRAFTY AT CAMOUFLAGE Mimicry is a wonderful form of camouflage and there is none better at this than the seadragon. Like all fish, seadragons have gills and fins. The fins

of seadragons are so fine that they are almost transparent. This makes them look leafy, which is the perfect camouflage for a life among the sea grasses. They even rock back and forth imitating the movement of the grasses by the ocean currents.

Like many species of seahorse, seadragons can change colour depending on their age, what they eat or even how stressed they are!

Many fish have scales, but not seadragons. They have a series of bony plates that cover their body. This 'armour' is great for protection but not good for easy movement which is why they rely mostly on their camouflage for their survival. They are slow swimmers, drifting and swimming in shallow waters, although they have been seen at depths of up to 50 metres.

AMAZING SEADRAGON FACTS

The Weedy Seadragon and the Leafy Seadragon are unique to Australia.

Seadragons are protected by law – it's illegal to take or export them without a permit.

Seadragons are under threat from their habitat being destroyed or polluted, and from those illegally collecting them for sale.

Sometimes seadragons can be found washed up on the beach, because their bony plates help to preserve them after death. Look closely in the clumps of weed because they may be camouflaged.

SEARCHING FOR DRAGONS

We don't know how long wild seadragons live, though it's thought they can live for five to seven years in captivity. As with all other fish, seadragons have ear bones that show growth rings. New growth rings appear throughout its life. So dead seadragons washed up on the beach can be very useful to researchers to perhaps be able to tell the age of the seadragon and so learn more about these fantastic Australian fish.

There is a seadragon monitoring program called Dragon Search which encourages members of the community to provide information on seadragon sightings. (www.dragonsearch.asn.au) The information is used to help find out more about where seadragons are found, the sort of habitat they need, and the kinds of things we might be able to do to help protect them. Anyone who visits the beach in Australia can get involved.

It is thought that seadragons may be sensitive to changes in water quality. So if the water quality becomes worse, the effect on populations of seadragons may be a warning signal that quick action needs to be taken. Frogs are used as a similar warning signal in freshwater environments.

30 wombat

bulldozer of the BUSH

They may look sleepy, docile and dozy but looks can be deceiving. Resting on the pathway or in the bush, the Common Wombat (*Vombatus ursinus*) looks as though it is dozing in the sunshine and it probably is, but disturb a wombat and it can run at an amazing speed – up to 40 kilometres per hour. That will only last for about 150 metres, then it will need a rest. Their doziness is one way of conserving energy by dropping their body temperature when they doze.

Another wonderful conservation method used by the wombat is to get almost all the moisture it needs from what it eats. So when it goes to the toilet its scats (that's poos!) are really dry. A wombat's droppings are easy to spot. They are usually a cube shape, about 2 centimetres long, dropped in a bundle of four to eight and lying out in the open. And the smudge on the rock nearby? That's where the wombat wiped its bottom! Wombats eat lots of grass, and when the grass supply is scarce, they dig for tubers and roots.

There are three species of wombat found in Australia, the Common Wombat, the Southern Hairy-nosed Wombat (*Lasiorhinus latifrons*) and the Northern Hairy-nosed Wombat (*Lasiorhinus krefftii*). As the name suggests, the nose or muzzle of a hairy-nosed wombat is covered with short brown hairs. Hairy-nosed wombats also have a wider face and longer, more pointed ears than a Common Wombat.

A QUADRUPED CALLED WOMBAT When early Europeans began exploring New Holland (Australia) they were intrigued and amazed by all the unique wildlife they were finding. Records were taken in the field and specimens were sent back to England for further study. These animals were unknown to science at the time.

One of the earliest descriptions of a wombat comes from George Bass (the man who circumnavigated Tasmania and the man after whom Bass Strait is named). His notes, written over 200 years ago, were titled 'Some Account of the Quadruped Called Wombat, in New South Wales' and his descriptions are wonderful. This is some of what he wrote from his observations of wombats at Furneaux Islands and from his discussions with a 'mountain native' about the 'wombat' living in the Blue Mountains behind the Sydney settlement:

The wombat ... is a squat, thick, shortlegged, and rather inactive quadruped with an appearance of great stumpy strength. Its figure and movements, if they do not resemble those of the bear, at least remind one of that animal ...

The head is large and flattish and, when looking the animal full in the face, seems, independent of the ears, to form nearly an equilateral triangle … The hair upon the face lies in regular order, as if combed with its ends pointed upwards in a kind of radii from the nose, their point of supposed junction.

Bass describes the mouth as small and the front of each jaw having two grass cutting teeth 'like those of the kangaroo'. The neck was thick and short, not allowing much movement and, according to Bass, 'looks rather as if it was stuck upon the shoulders'. The 'size of the two sexes are nearly the same' with the female being a little heavier. Bass described the wombat's movement as 'hobbling or shuffling, like the awkward gait of the bear', and said that most men could outrun a wombat.

He described the voice of a wombat as 'a low cry between a hissing and a whizzing' that was only ever uttered in anger and could only be heard for 25 or 35 metres. For Bass the wombat appeared mild and gentle. He was even able to carry the wombat for a mile in his arms and on his shoulders just like humans carry their babies. Bass also tied a wombat's legs together so that it wouldn't shuffle away. Today we consider this inappropriate, but back then it was part of the process of observing the animal. He soon found out that the gentle wombat can become very annoyed when provoked as it 'whizzed with all his might, kicked and scratched most furiously and snapped off a piece from the elbow of my jacket with his long grass cutters'.

EXPERT EXCAVATORS In Bass's time no one had yet opened a burrow to look inside. Today people have even crawled inside a wombat's burrow and we know much more. Wombats don't just have one burrow, they have many burrows and some may reach up to 20 metres or more underground and two metres below the surface. There will be nesting chambers

and connecting tunnels. And there is usually more than one entrance to the burrow system. A wombat's hard bony bottom is great protection in a burrow. They can block the entrance or crush a predator against the burrow walls. Wombat burrows also offer fantastic protection from weather extremes and bushfires.

Wombats are mainly solitary and nocturnal, coming up when the air is cool to graze on their favourite foods – native grasses. On summer days they will usually stay in their burrows to escape the heat but in winter they will often come out to bask in sun.

Wombats have feet wonderfully adapted for digging. They also have a backward opening pouch (just like its koala relative), which stops it getting full of dirt when the wombat digs. In the pouch there are two teats but usually only one young is born. The joey will live in the pouch for 6 months and then stay with the mother until it is 18 months old. If there is plenty of food, wombats can breed throughout the year.

For wombats their biggest threat lies with humans – our destruction of their habitat, introduction of animals that compete for food, and our cars!

RARER THAN THE GIANT PANDA!

The Northern Hairy-nosed Wombat is one of the rarest animals in the world and is classified as critically endangered. There is only one small group left in the Epping Forest National Park in central Queensland. They were once found as far south as the Victorian border but their numbers became drastically reduced due to drought, clearing of land for farming, and competition for food from introduced rabbits, sheep and cattle. The Epping Forest population got down to as few as 35 animals but once the park was fenced from cattle and sheep, and later from dingos, numbers built up to over 100 – still a very fragile situation. Researchers are trying to find out as much as they can about this hairy-nosed hermit so that they can help the present population to increase and hopefully establish new populations elsewhere.

AMAZING WOMBAT FACTS

🐗 The Common Wombat's scientific name is *Vombatus ursinus*. *Vombatus* is possibly derived from the aboriginal names for wombat: 'wambad', 'wambaj' or 'wambag'. *Ursinus* is latin for 'bear-like'.

🐗 Wombats have long front teeth for chewing – a bit like a rodent's. The tough grasses they eat wear their teeth down, but luckily a wombat's teeth never stop growing so it can still grind its food even when it's old.

🐗 Wombats are the largest burrowing herbivorous marsupial.

🐗 It is for good reason that the wombat is called the bulldozer of the bush. Most fences are no trouble for a wombat on a mission. They simply will bulldoze straight through the fence and leave another hole to be repaired.

🐗 The wombat's nearest living relative is the koala.

🐗 Wombats can live to 15 years in the wild, and up to 20 years in captivity.

guys, girls, bubs and the whole gang!

Here are some great names used to describe the males, females, young and groups of some of our amazing Australian animals.

ANIMAL	MALE	FEMALE	YOUNG	COLLECTIVE NOUN
Bird (general)	Cock	Hen	Hatchling, chick	Dissimulation (small birds only), fleet, flight, flock, parcel, pod, volery
Brumby/horse	Stallion	Mare	Foal, colt or filly	Stud, team, herd
Camel	Bull	Cow	Calf	Herd
Cane Toad/ toad (general)				Knot (for toads)
Cicada			Nymph	
Crocodile			Hatchling	
Death Adder/ Snake (general)			Snakelets, neonate (newly born) hatchling (newly hatched)	Lair, den, slither, nest, pit
Dingo/dog	Dog	Bitch	Pup, whelp	Litter (pups from one mother), pack (hunting), kennel, colony
Dugong	Bull	Cow	Pup, calf	Herd, pod, school
Echidna	Male	Female	Puggle	Train (in mating season)

Emu	Cock	Hen	Chick	Flock, mob
Fish (general)	Male	Female	Fingerling, fry	School, shoal, draft, run
Ghost Bat	Male	Female	Pup	Colony
Great White Shark/shark (general)	Male	Female	Cub	School, shiver
Green and Golden Bell Frog/frog (general)	Male	Female	Tadpole, polliwog	Army, knot, croak
Kangaroo	Jack, buck, boomer	Jill, doe, flyer	Joey	Mob, troop, herd
Koala	Boar	Sow	Cub	Group, colony, sleep
Kookaburra				Watch (for kingfishers)
Lake Eacham Rainbowfish/ rainbowfish (general)			Fingerling, fry	School, shoal, party
Little Penguin			Chick	Colony, rookery
Rabbit	Buck	Doe	Kit, kitten	Colony, nest
Redback Spider			Spiderling	
Sulphur-crested Cockatoo				Flock, company (for parrots)
Weedy Seadragon				Herd (seahorses)
Wombat	Jack	Jill	Joey	

Not all animals have been assigned particular names for the sex of the animal; many are simply male or female. Some animals do have a collective name for a group while others that are not usually found in groups don't.

Here are some other really awesome collective nouns for animals:

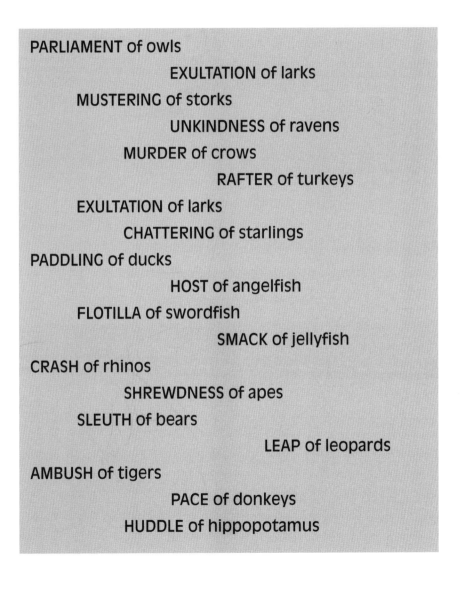

PARLIAMENT of owls

EXULTATION of larks

MUSTERING of storks

UNKINDNESS of ravens

MURDER of crows

RAFTER of turkeys

EXULTATION of larks

CHATTERING of starlings

PADDLING of ducks

HOST of angelfish

FLOTILLA of swordfish

SMACK of jellyfish

CRASH of rhinos

SHREWDNESS of apes

SLEUTH of bears

LEAP of leopards

AMBUSH of tigers

PACE of donkeys

HUDDLE of hippopotamus

Animal Emblems of Australia

Aust. Capital Territory

Mammal: No official emblem
Bird: Gang-gang Cockatoo (*Callocephalon fimbriatum*)
Marine: No official emblem

New South Wales

Mammal: Platypus (*Ornithorhynchus anatinus*)
Bird: Kookaburra (*Dacelo novaeguineae*)
Marine: Eastern Blue Groper (*Achoerodus viridis*)

Northern Territory

Mammal: Red Kangaroo (*Macropus rufus*)
Bird: Wedge-tailed Eagle (*Aquila audax*)
Marine: No official emblem

Queensland

Mammal: Koala (*Phascolarctos cinereus*)
Bird: Brolga (*Grus rubicundus*)
Marine: Barrier Reef Anemonefish (*Amphiprion akindynos*)

South Australia

Mammal: Southern Hairy-nosed Wombat (*Lasiorhinus latifrons*)
Bird: Piping Shrike, also known as White-backed Magpie (*Gymnorhina tibicen leuconota*) (unofficial). Appears on state badge.
Marine: Leafy Seadragon (*Phycodurus eques*)

Tasmania

Mammal: Tasmanian Devil (*Sarcophilus harrisii*) (unofficial)
Bird: No bird emblem, but the Yellow Wattlebird (*Anthochaera paradoxa*) is generally acknowledged to be their most identifiable bird.
Marine: No official emblem

Victoria

Mammal: Leadbeater's Possum (*Gymnobelideus leadbeateri*)
Bird: Helmeted Honeyeater (*Lichenostomus melanops cassidix*)
Marine: Weedy Seadragon (*Phyllopteryx taeniolatus*)

Western Australia

Mammal: Numbat (*Myrmecobius fasciatus*)
Bird: Black Swan (*Cygnus atratus*)
Marine: No official emblem

How to find out more

Thankfully we have many organisations in Australia that promote our amazing animals.

Check out your local state or territory museum, government environment and parks and wildlife organisations, and don't forget that our zoos are a fantastic source of information about our native animals – they display many of the smaller species (including the nocturnal ones) that you will rarely see in the wild. You might even want to become an official friend of your zoo!

SOME ORGANISATIONS AND WEBSITES ARE:

Australian Faunal Directory: http://www.environment.gov.au/biodiversity/abrs/ online-resources/fauna/afd

Australian Museum: http://www.amonline.net.au

Australian Regional Association of Zoological Parks and Aquaria: http://www.arazpa.org.au

Cephalopod Page: http://www.thecephalopodpage.org

CSIRO and especially the biodiversity and ecology link: http://www.csiro.au/csiro/channel/ich2u.html

Department of Environment and Water Resources: http://www.environment.gov.au/biodiversity/index.html

Frog and Tadpole Study Group: http://www.fats.org.au

Frog Watch: http://www.frogwatch.org.au

Museum of Victoria: http://www.museum.vic.gov.au

Science in the News NOVA: http://www.science.org.au/nova/index.htm

References

Australian Regional Association of Zoological Parks and Aquaria Animal Fact Sheets: http://www.arazpa.org.au/default.aspx?ArticleID =66

Australian State of the Environment 2006 (SoE2006) report: http://www.deh.gov.au/soe/2006

Cogger, Harold; *Reptiles and Amphibians of Australia*; Reed Books; 1992

Fleay, David; *We Breed the Platypus*; Robertson and Mullens, 1944

Museum of Victoria: 'Caught & Coloured: Zoological Illustrations from Colonial Victoria', collection of Frederick McCoy's *Prodromus of the Zoology of Victoria*: http://www.museum.vic.gov.au/caughtandcoloured/Zoology.aspx

National Library of Australia and their collections including: 'The World Upside Down', National Library of Australia: http://www.nla.gov.au/exhibitions/upsidedown/index.html Perry, George; *Arcana; or the Museum of Natural History*, London, 1811

Reader's Digest Complete Book of Australian Birds; Reader's Digest; first ed (2nd revised); 1983

State Library of NSW and their collections including: the papers of Sir Joseph Banks: http://www.sl.nsw.gov.au/banks/series_35/35_43.cfm and the papers of John Harris, 1791–1837: http://image.sl.nsw.gov.au/Ebind/cy157/a1369/a1369000.html

Strahan, Ronald (ed); *The Australian Museum Complete Book of Australian Mammals*; Angus and Robertson, 1983

Christopher Cheng worked as a teacher in city and country schools before moving to Taronga Zoo as an education officer for 8 years, establishing Australia's first Zoomobile. He has been National Children's Development Manager at Dymocks, and Education Advisor for the BioScope Initiative, a science based CDROM project at Purdue University, USA.

He is an accomplished children's author, now writing full time, conducting workshops and visiting schools. He has also presented to students at schools and universities in the USA. Chris writes both fiction and non fiction. His picture book *One Child* (illustrated by Steven Woolman) won the Wilderness Society Environment Award for Picture Books (Australia) and the 2000 Skipping Stones Honour Book (USA).

Chris has a Master of Arts in Children's Literature and is also the Literacy Ambassador for the Federal Government's Literacy and Numeracy Week Initiative.

Chris lives in Sydney, Australia, near wonderful coffee shops and restaurants in a very old (newly renovated) terrace with his wife.

Find out more about Chris at: www.chrischeng.com

Gregory Rogers studied fine art at the Queensland College of Art and has illustrated a large number of educational and trade children's picture books including four books in the Random House *30 Australian . . .* series. In 1995 he won the Kate Greenaway Medal for his illustrations in *Way Home*, a book that also won a Parent's Choice Award in the US and was shortlisted for the ABPA book design awards.

His first wordless picture book *The Boy, the Bear, the Baron, the Bard* was selected as one of the Ten Best Illustrated Picture Books of 2004 by the *New York Times* and short-listed for the CBCA Awards, Younger Readers, 2005 and the APA Best Designed Children's Picture Book, 2004. It also received a 2004 Australian and New Zealand Illustration Award from Illustrators Australia and was a Notable Children's Book of the Year for the American Library Association. His second wordless picture book, *Midsummer Knight*, was published in 2006. It is the companion to *The Boy, The Bear, The Baron, The Bard* and is also published in the USA, France and Germany.

Gregory lives in Brisbane, Australia. He shares a cluttered, old house with his partner and two cats.